英语1知识点强化练习

主　编　黄静静　李国辉　周巍巍
副主编　郭亚辉　薛鸿燕

北京理工大学出版社
BEIJING INSTITUTE OF TECHNOLOGY PRESS

版权专有　侵权必究

图书在版编目(CIP)数据

英语1知识点强化练习 / 黄静静，李国辉，周巍巍主编. -- 北京：北京理工大学出版社，2023.5
ISBN 978-7-5763-2428-0

Ⅰ.①英… Ⅱ.①黄… ②李… ③周… Ⅲ.①英语课-中等专业学校-升学参考资料 Ⅳ.①G634.413

中国国家版本馆 CIP 数据核字(2023)第 097099 号

出版发行 / 北京理工大学出版社有限责任公司
社　　址 / 北京市海淀区中关村南大街5号
邮　　编 / 100081
电　　话 / (010)68914775(总编室)
　　　　　 (010)82562903(教材售后服务热线)
　　　　　 (010)68944723(其他图书服务热线)
网　　址 / http://www.bitpress.com.cn
经　　销 / 全国各地新华书店
印　　刷 / 定州市新华印刷有限公司
开　　本 / 787毫米×1092毫米　1/16
印　　张 / 11　　　　　　　　　　　　　　责任编辑 / 武丽娟
字　　数 / 225千字　　　　　　　　　　　　文案编辑 / 武丽娟
版　　次 / 2023年5月第1版　2023年5月第1次印刷　　责任校对 / 刘亚男
定　　价 / 35.00元　　　　　　　　　　　　责任印制 / 边心超

图书出现印装质量问题，请拨打售后服务热线，本社负责调换

前　言

本书依据《中等职业学校英语课程标准（2020年版）》，结合中等职业学校就业与升学的实际情况而编写。

本书能够夯实学生的英语学习基础，适用于所有中职学生的英语学习。共分为8个单元，每个单元所附的习题，以 Warming up、Listening and Speaking、Reading and Writing、Grammar 以及 For Better Performance 五个模块的形式展开，呈现方式多样化，以语音、填空、选择、对话练习、完形填空、阅读理解、改错及写作的练习方式帮助学生掌握词汇、课文内容和语法知识，使其拓展知识面，提高英语水平。针对学生高考的需求，在每个单元的学习内容结束后，本书又附有单元检测习题，习题内容符合对口英语高考大纲，且题型与高考题型一致，能有效地达到举一反三、灵活运用所学知识点的目的，可以帮助学生在日常学习中巩固基础、提高技能。本书很好地满足了职业学校的学生参加职教高考的需求。

我们本着"注重基础，突出运用，精选内容，强化训练，提高分数"的原则，力争做到"由浅入深、循序渐进"，符合中等职业学校学生的认知特点和接受能力。本书可作为中等职业学校教师的复习教学用书，也可作为一、二年级学生日常学习用书，而对于参加对口升学的毕业班学生来说，其同样适用。

本书的作者均是来自教学一线、有多年教学经验的教师。但由于水平有限，疏漏与不足之处在所难免，恳请各位老师、同学及其他读者批评指正。

编　者

目 录

Unit 1　Personal and Family Life ·· 1
　Warming up ··· 1
　Listening and Speaking ·· 2
　Reading and Writing ·· 3
　Grammar ·· 5
　For Better Performance ·· 8
　单元检测 ·· 9

Unit 2　Transportation ·· 18
　Warming up ··· 18
　Listening and Speaking ·· 19
　Reading and Writing ·· 20
　Grammar ·· 23
　For Better Performance ·· 26
　单元检测 ·· 27

Unit 3　Shopping ··· 36
　Warming up ··· 36
　Listening and Speaking ·· 37
　Reading and Writing ·· 39
　Grammar ·· 41
　For Better Performance ·· 44
　单元检测 ·· 46

Unit 4　School Life ·· 54
　Warming up ··· 54
　Listening and Speaking ·· 55
　Reading and Writing ·· 57
　Grammar ·· 60

For Better Performance ··· 63
  单元检测 ··· 64

Unit 5 Celebrations ·· 73
  Warming up ··· 73
  Listening and Speaking ··· 74
  Reading and Writing ··· 75
  Grammar ··· 78
  For Better Performance ··· 81
  单元检测 ··· 82

Unit 6 Food and Drinks ·· 91
  Warming up ··· 91
  Listening and Speaking ··· 92
  Reading and Writing ··· 93
  Grammar ··· 96
  For Better Performance ·· 100
  单元检测 ·· 101

Unit 7 The Internet ·· 110
  Warming up ·· 110
  Listening and Speaking ·· 111
  Reading and Writing ·· 112
  Grammar ·· 115
  For Better Performance ·· 118
  单元检测 ·· 119

Unit 8 People and Events ·· 128
  Warming up ·· 128
  Listening and Speaking ·· 129
  Reading and Writing ·· 130
  Grammar ·· 133
  For Better Performance ·· 136
  单元检测 ·· 137

Unit 1

Personal and Family Life

Warming up

一、句型汇总

1. I'm a delivery person. Fan is my given name. 我是一名送货员。Fan 是我的名字。

2. I'm a flight attendant. How can I help you. 我是一名空姐。我能帮你什么忙吗?

3. I work as a teacher in Star Vocational High School. 我在明星职业高中当老师。

4. Could you tell me something about your family? 你能和我谈谈你的家庭吗?

5. Emma and I are planning to hold a party for her. Emma 和我计划为她举办一个派对。

6. In formal situations, we usually use Mr, Mrs or Ms before a family name. 在正式的场合我们经常把 Mr、Mrs 和 Ms 放在姓氏的前面。

7. Few Chinese people name their children after famous people. 很少有中国人以名人来命名他们的孩子。

二、英汉互译

1. community _____
2. energetic _____
3. especially _____
4. introduce _____
5. manager _____
6. vocational _____
7. 礼物_____
8. 小狗_____
9. 谈论_____
10. 节日_____
11. 姓氏_____

Listening and Speaking

一、找出与所给单词画线部分读音相同的选项

( )1. comm<u>u</u>nity   A. p<u>u</u>ppy   B. intr<u>o</u>duce   C. p<u>u</u>ll   D. incl<u>u</u>de

( )2. v<u>o</u>cational   A. n<u>o</u>tice   B. j<u>o</u>g   C. intr<u>o</u>duce   D. c<u>u</u>stom

( )3. c<u>oo</u>k   A. fl<u>oo</u>d   B. f<u>oo</u>d   C. w<u>oo</u>d   D. c<u>oo</u>l

( )4. <u>i</u>ntroduce   A. f<u>a</u>mily   B. v<u>i</u>sit   C. h<u>i</u>gh   D. sm<u>i</u>le

( )5. <u>e</u>nergetic   A. b<u>e</u>lieve   B. <u>e</u>ducation   C. compl<u>e</u>te   D. <u>e</u>special

二、从 B 栏中找出与 A 栏中相对应的答语

A	B
1. Could you please introduce yourself?	A. She comes from Liverpool, a city in England.
2. Where is your mother from?	B. My name is Li Jia.
3. What is your father's job?	C. Yes, they live here.
4. Is it your brother?	D. He works as a manager in a big company.
5. Do they also live in this community?	E. No, it is my sister.

三、用所给句子补全下面对话

A：Could you tell me something about your family?

B：Sure. 1

A：He's very strong. Is he a football player?

B：No. 2 He manages a department. But he likes playing football.

A：Who is this baby in your mother's arms? 3

B：No, it's my sister. 4

A：I see. And this little boy must be you.

B：Bingo! 5

A. He's a manager.

B. Is it your brother?

C. This man holding a football is my father.

D. She's a primary school student now.

E. I was only six years old then.

四、场景模拟

编写一组对话,向你的妈妈介绍你的好朋友。

提示词汇:this is…　come from　work as　hardworking　get on well with

Reading and Writing

一、用括号内所给汉语提示或单词的适当形式填空

1. Our grandparents live in the same _____ (社区).

2. My grandma is _____ (精力充沛的).

3. But they are also strict with us, _____ (尤其是) about our homework.

4. Chongyang Festival is coming. We are preparing a _____ (手工制作的) gift for them.

5. My parents go _____ (慢跑) every evening.

6. He _____ (经营) a department.

7. I live with my _____ (父母) and my younger sister.

8. My parents are _____ (严格的) with us, especially about our homework.

9. We are _____ (prepare) a handmade gift for them.

10. Children in English speaking countries may be _____ (name) after their parents.

二、完形填空

Hello, everyone. My name is Diana Hill. My first name is Diana. Hill is my __1__ name. I am __2__ English girl. I am 12 years old. There are __3__ people in my family. They are my parents, my two brothers __4__ I. I also have a cousin. She is my uncle's __5__. We play ping-pong every day. We like it very much.

Look! This is a photo __6__ my new room. There is a big bed. It's __7__. A desk is between the pink bed and the red sofa. My computer and CDs __8__ on the desk. My books are in the bookcase. __9__ is my schoolbag? Is it on the chair? No, it's __10__ the chair. Oh, who did it? My dog Lucky, of course.

( ) 1. A. first   B. middle   C. family   D. school
( ) 2. A. a   B. an   C. the   D. /
( ) 3. A. four   B. five   C. six   D. seven
( ) 4. A. but   B. and   C. or   D. so
( ) 5. A. son   B. brother   C. daughter D. sister
( ) 6. A. of   B. for   C. to   D. from
( ) 7. A. red   B. blue   C. pink   D. white
( ) 8. A. be   B. am   C. is   D. are
( ) 9. A. What   B. Who   C. How   D. Where
( ) 10. A. on   B. in   C. under   D. /

三、阅读理解

阅读下面短文,从每题所给的 A、B、C、D 四个选项中选出最佳答案。

Everyone has a family name. In China, the family name is the first name, but in English-speaking countries the family name is the last name. Do you know how English people get their family names?

Some family names come from the places of their homes. For example, a man lives on or near a hill, then his family name may be Hill. In England, people's family names may be Wood, Lake, because they live near the wood or the lake.

Some family names come from a person's job. If a person is a cook, his family name may be Cook.

And many people get their family names from their fathers' names. If you hear the name "Jackson", you can know that he is the son of Jack.

( ) 1. The passage is about _____.

　　A. first names　　B. English family　　C. given names　　D. family names

( ) 2. In the passage, English people usually have _____ ways to get their family names.

　　A. one　　B. two　　C. three　　D. four

( ) 3. A man lives near the lake. His family name may be _____.

　　A. Hill　　B. Wood　　C. Lake　　D. Cook

( ) 4. Jack's family name is Cook. His family name may come from the _____.

　　A. place　　B. job　　C. country　　D. hobby

( ) 5. Which of the following is WRONG?

　　A. Everyone has a family name.

　　B. Family names are the same between China and England.

　　C. Jackson may be the son of Jack.

　　D. Hill, Lake, Cook are the last names in England.

四、书面表达

以"My best friend"为题,写一篇文章,介绍一下你的好朋友(80~100 词)。

_____
_____
_____
_____
_____
_____

Grammar

一、从下面每小题四个选项中选出最佳选项

( ) 1. —_____ he _____ in China?

　　— No, he _____.

　　A. Does; live; not live　　B. Does; lives; doesn't

　　C. Does; live; doesn't　　D. Do; live; don't

(　　) 2. The Earth _____ around the Sun.
　　　　A. go　　　　　B. went　　　　C. goes　　　　D. will go

(　　) 3. My father is a doctor. He _____ on Saturday or Sunday.
　　　　A. not work　　B. isn't working　C. don't work　　D. doesn't work

(　　) 4. —Be quiet, please! The baby _____.
　　　　—Sorry.
　　　　A. sleeps　　　B. slept　　　　C. is sleeping　　D. was sleeping

(　　) 5. The students _____ games after class. They _____ volleyball over there now.
　　　　A. play; are playing　　　　　B. are playing; play
　　　　C. plays; is playing　　　　　D. is playing; plays

(　　) 6. —What does your brother often do on Saturday morning?
　　　　—He often _____ basketball with his friends.
　　　　A. plays　　　B. play　　　　C. is playing　　D. are playing

(　　) 7. Chinese food _____ to be healthy by most people.
　　　　A. is considered　B. considers　　C. is considering　D. has considered

(　　) 8. My father is a bus driver. He always _____ up very early.
　　　　A. get　　　　B. got　　　　　C. gets　　　　　D. will get

(　　) 9. _____ your brother always _____ hard?
　　　　A. Do; work　　B. Does; works　C. Is; work　　　D. Does; work

(　　) 10. Alice often _____ to English on the Internet.
　　　　A. listen　　　B. listens　　　C. is listening　　D. are listening

(　　) 11. If Mary _____, she will succeed in passing the exam.
　　　　A. will work hard　　　　　　B. works hard
　　　　C. works hardly　　　　　　　D. will work hardly

(　　) 12. His friend _____ a yellow hat.
　　　　A. doesn't have　B. don't have　C. does have　　D. have

(　　) 13. Many foreigners _____ to visit Beijing every year.
　　　　A. come　　　B. came　　　　C. comes　　　　D. will come

(　　) 14. Mr. Smith often _____ short stories, but he is writing a TV play these days.
　　　　A. is writing　B. was writing　C. writes　　　　D. wrote

(　　) 15. In China, red _____ good luck.
　　　　A. means　　　B. mean　　　　C. is meaning　　D. meaning

(　　) 16. The library _____ at 2 every afternoon, so I think it _____ now.

A. opens; opens B. opens; is open
C. is open; opens D. is open; open

( ) 17. Kitty _____, and she looks very beautiful.
A. have long hairs B. has long hair
C. has long hairs D. have long hair

( ) 18. —What _____ they _____ of Amanda?
—They love her.
A. do; think B. are; think C. does; think D. is; thinking

( ) 19. My friend _____ at six.
A. get B. get up C. getting up D. gets up

( ) 20. Listen! Someone _____ an English song now.
A. sings B. sang C. is singing D. was singing

( ) 21. We often _____ on the playground.
A. play B. playing C. plays D. played

( ) 22. _____ he brush his teeth every morning?
A. Do B. Does C. Did D. Doing

( ) 23. What _____ Amy and Sara do after school?
A. do B. does C. did D. doing

( ) 24. Tom and his sister _____ the same hobby.
A. have B. has C. had D. having

( ) 25. My dog runs fast, _____ he?
A. does B. doesn't C. did D. didn't

( ) 26. Chrissy doesn't _____ her party at home.
A. enjoy B. enjoys C. enjoying D. enjoyed

( ) 27. He, together with his parents, _____ and _____ dinner at home on Saturdays.
A. cook; have B. cooks; has
C. cooked; had D. cooking; having

( ) 28. I learned that the Earth _____ around the Sun when I was eight.
A. go B. going C. went D. goes

( ) 29. The football commentator shouts out: "He _____ the ball! It flies into the gate."
A. kick B. kicked C. kicks D. kicking

( ) 30. The train _____ at the station at 9:30 according to the timetable.

A. arrive　　　B. arrives　　　C. arrived　　　D. is arriving

二、找出下列句子中错误的选项，并改正过来

1. My father didn't enjoy to do housework after work.
　　　　　　　A　　　B　　C　　　　D

2. As time goes by, the weather become hotter and hotter.
　A　　　B　　　　　　　　C　　　　D

3. The teacher said light traveled faster than sound.
　　　　　　A　　　　B　　　C　　D

4. He will come to see me if he will have time tomorrow.
　　　A　　　　B　　　C　　D

5. Does your mother wants to go shopping on the vacation?
　A　　　　　　　B　　C　　　　　　D

6. Tom doesn't does his homework after school.
　　　A　　　B　　C　　　　D

7. What time do Lily go to school every morning?
　　A　　B　　　　　　C　　D

8. Don't comes here with me tomorrow, please.
　　A　　B　　　　　　C　　　　　　D

9. Tom has hardly finished his homework, hasn't he?
　　A　　　B　　　　　C　　　　　D

10. What a fine weather it was yesterday!
　　　A　　B　　　C　　　D

For Better Performance

一、找出与所给单词画线部分读音相同的选项

1. community　　A. introduce　　B. jog　　C. note　　D. photo

2. family　　　　A. handmade　　B. manager　　C. vocation　　D. game

3. weight　　　　A. laugh　　　　B. enough　　C. rough　　　D. straight

4. puppy　　　　A. introduce　　B. music　　C. community　　D. cut

5. child　　　　A. visit　　　　B. unique　　C. life　　　D. gift

二、英汉互译

1. 对……严格的 _____　　　2. 高中 _____

3. 妹妹 _____　　　　　　　4. 职业学校 _____

5. 尤其是 _____　　　　　　6. handmade _____

7. work as _____
8. delivery person _____
9. take care of _____
10. pay attention to _____

三、用括号内所给汉语提示或单词的适当形式填空

1. Ella Baker, one of my friends is a _____ (deliver) person.
2. This man _____ (hold) a basketball is my father.
3. They are also strict with us, _____ (especial) about our homework.
4. The 13-year-old boy is creative and _____ (energy).
5. My grandfather _____ (live) alone in his own house.
6. Let me _____ (介绍) my best friend Kate to you.
7. I never knew you could make such delicious _____ (手工的) noodles.
8. I live with my parents and my _____ (年轻的) sister.
9. The given name means _____ (教育) the young.
10. Your doctor can tell you something about _____ (慢跑).

四、找出下列句子中错误的选项,并改正过来

1. The bottle is filled of water.
      A   B   C   D

2. Help you to some fruit, girls.
      A   B C   D

3. Our library is big, but your library is bigger than our.
     A   B   C   D

4. Parents should not be strict of their teenagers.
      A   B   C   D

5. Do you know what do this word means?
      A   B   C   D

单元检测

第一部分 英语知识运用(共分三节,满分40分)

第一节 语音知识:从 A、B、C、D 四个选项中找出其画线部分与所给单词画线部分读音相同的选项。(共5分,每小题1分)

(　　) 1. climb　　A. energetic　　B. notice　　C. introduce　　D. city

(　　) 2. manager　　A. vocation　　B. stomach　　C. family　　D. handmade

(   )3. gift   A. visit   B. light   C. high   D. website

(   )4. parent   A. manage   B. thing   C. think   D. saying

(   )5. hardly   A. forward   B. warm   C. popular   D. garden

第二节　词汇与语法知识：从 A、B、C、D 四个选项中选出可以填入空白处的最佳选项。（共 25 分，每小题 1 分）

(   )6. — Nice to meet you.
　　　— _____.
　　A. Good morning   B. Happy to see you
　　C. Nice to meet you, too   D. Pleased to see you

(   )7. Our teacher is strict _____ us _____ everything.
　　A. in; with   B. in; in   C. with; with   D. with; in

(   )8. My elder brother is _____, because he goes jogging every morning.
　　A. lazy   B. happy   C. energetic   D. strict

(   )9. I am so happy that my grandparents live in the same _____. We can look after each other.
　　A. manager   B. community   C. gift   D. company

(   )10. In the picture, my mom is holding a baby in _____ arms.
　　A. she's   B. his   C. her   D. hers

(   )11. Susan doesn't _____ her parents any more; she is an adult now.
　　A. live alone   B. live with   C. live together D. live off

(   )12. In China, many parents are _____ with their children, especially about homework.
　　A. strict   B. sad   C. happy   D. energetic

(   )13. My fourteen-year-old sister is now studying in a _____ school.
　　A. vocation   B. vocational C. vacation   D. vacational

(   )14. — _____ is your mother?
　　　— My mother is a teacher at a primary school.
　　A. What   B. Who   C. How   D. When

(   )15. The West Lake is quite popular among visitors across the world, _____ in summer and winter.
　　A. special   B. specially   C. especial   D. especially

(   )16. Fred is always _____ because he often does something good for his health outdoors.
　　A. weak   B. nervous   C. serious   D. energetic

Unit 1 Personal and Family Life

(   )17. —I'm afraid Mr. White doesn't know me.

—Don't worry. I _____ you to him when we meet.

A. introduce   B. introduced   C. will introduce   D. have introduced

(   )18. It's very late. You'd better _____ alone in the street.

A. don't jog   B. not jogging   C. not jog   D. not to jog

(   )19. The boss made him _____ for twelve hours a day.

A. work   B. worked   C. to work   D. works

(   )20. Her name is Kate Joan Green. Kate is her _____.

A. family name   B. given name   C. full name   D. middle name

(   )21. When I _____ at the airport, I _____ you on the phone.

A. reach; will tell   B. reach; tell

C. arrive; will tell   D. arrive; tell

(   )22. —What _____ Yu Ping usually _____ after school?

—She usually goes to the library.

A. does; do   B. is; doing   C. does; does   D. do; does

(   )23. She is _____ and she has an _____ brother.

A. ten-year-old; eight years old   B. ten-year-old; eight-year-old

C. ten-years-old; eight years old   D. ten years old; eight-year-old

(   )24. The students are busy _____ for the English reading competition.

A. prepare   B. to prepare   C. prepared   D. preparing

(   )25. Can you help me _____ my English?

A. with   B. of   C. learning   D. about

(   )26. The students _____ the trip to the Great Wall the day after tomorrow.

A. will plan   B. are going to plan

C. are planning to   D. are planning

(   )27. The little girl asked her father why the earth _____ around the sun.

A. travels   B. travel   C. traveled   D. will travel

(   )28. —Thank you for helping me with my English.

—_____.

A. All right.   B. OK

C. You're welcome   D. No thanks

(   )29. —_____ will you come back?

—In three days.

A. How often   B. How long   C. How soon   D. How far

— 11 —

(   )30. _____ happy time we have these days!
　　　　A. What　　　B. What a　　　C. How　　　D. How a

第三节　完形填空：阅读下面的短文，从所给的 **A**、**B**、**C**、**D** 四个选项中选出正确的答案。(共 10 分,每小题 1 分)

　　People in English speaking countries put given name before family name. But many Chinese always put family name before ___31___ name. Family names are so ___32___ to us because they tell who our ancestors are and where we are from. ___33___, the ways of addressing people are the same in English and in Chinese. We can ___34___ people by their full names. For example, Zhong Nanshan and George Washington. In ___35___ situations, we usually use Mr, Mrs or Ms before a family name. For example, Mr Zhong and Mr Washington. And between close friends, we can ___36___ given names. For example, George.

　　___37___ naming children, in ___38___ speaking countries children may be named after their parents or grandparents. And some parents name their children ___39___ famous people. In China, however, you can ___40___ find anyone having the same given name as their parents or grandparents. And few Chinese people name their children after famous people.

(　　)31. A. last　　　　B. given　　　　C. second　　　　D. full
(　　)32. A. important　　B. easy　　　　C. convenient　　D. interesting
(　　)33. A. Therefore　　B. Because　　 C. Though　　　　D. However
(　　)34. A. watch　　　 B. move　　　　C. address　　　 D. stay
(　　)35. A. happy　　　 B. formal　　　 C. lucky　　　　 D. many
(　　)36. A. play　　　　B. write　　　　C. use　　　　　D. get
(　　)37. A. As for　　　B. As per　　　 C. As soon　　　D. As long
(　　)38. A. Chinese　　 B. Japanese　　 C. China's　　　D. English
(　　)39. A. after　　　 B. of　　　　　C. with　　　　 D. for
(　　)40. A. often　　　 B. never　　　 C. hardly　　　 D. ever

第二部分　篇章与词汇理解(共分三节,满分 50 分)

第一节　阅读理解：阅读下列短文,从每题所给的 **A**、**B**、**C**、**D** 四个选项中,选出最恰当的答案。(共 30 分,每小题 2 分)

A

　　It was a fine morning. At 7:30, Carlos went to his friend's home. He knocked at the door. "Hey, Bob! Come on!" he called. Carlos waited for three minutes. Then he knocked at the door again. At last the door opened. Bob came out. He looked like he was sleeping. He was putting his coat on and getting some books.

Unit 1 Personal and Family Life

"Wake up, Bob!" said Carlos. "What's the matter with you?"

Bob opened one eye. "Well, I watched TV last night. It was very late, but it was a very good film. It was about spies(间谍). I like it very much."

"Come on!" Carlos said. "Now we are late for school." Carlos pushed open the door and they went to school.

"Hey, look at that!" said Carlos.

Bob turned and looked. "Oh, wow!" said Bob.

A wounded(受伤的) man was coming to them. Bob and Carlos saw some blood(血) on that man's coat and trousers. The man stopped when he saw the boys.

"Help!" he said, "Help me!"

Carlos took Bob's arm. "We had better get out of here. That man looks like trouble!"

The boys wanted to run away. But the wounded man ran to the boys when a black car was coming.

(　　)41. Carlos and Bob were _____.
　　　A. policemen　　B. workers　　C. teachers　　D. students

(　　)42. Carlos knocked at Bob's door. Bob _____.
　　　A. got up at once
　　　B. didn't get up all the time
　　　C. didn't get up until three minutes later
　　　D. went to bed again

(　　)43. Bob liked the film on TV very much because it was about _____.
　　　A. doctors　　B. spies　　C. a wounded man　　D. policemen

(　　)44. "That man looks like trouble!" here means _____.
　　　A. He doesn't look well　　　　B. He needs some help
　　　C. He may be a bad man　　　　D. He wants to help us

(　　)45. The black car _____.
　　　A. saw Bob and Carlos
　　　B. found some blood on the man's coat and trousers
　　　C. ran to the boys
　　　D. were running after the man

B

In almost every big university in the United States, football is a favorite sport. American football is different. Players sometimes kick the ball, but they also throw the ball and run with it. They try to take it to the other end of the field. They have four chances to move the ball ten yards

(码). They can carry it or they can throw it. If they move the ball ten yards, they can try to move it another ten yards. If they move it to the end of the field, they receive six points(点).

It is difficult to move the ball. Eleven men on the other team try to stop the man with the ball. If he does not move the ball ten yards, his team kicks the ball to the other team.

Each university wants its own team to win. Many thousands of people come to watch. They all shout for their favorite team.

Young men and women come on the field to help the people shout more. They dance and jump while they shout. Each team plays ten or eleven games each season. The season begins in September and ends in November. If a team is very good, it may play another game after the season ends. The best teams play again on January 1, the first day of the New Year. Many people go to see these games and many others watch them on TV.

(　　)46. The passage talks about _____.

  A. football   B. how to play football

  C. American sports   D. American football

(　　)47. We can _____ the football in both American football and Chinese football.

  A. kick   B. throw   C. run with   D. catch

(　　)48. Why is it difficult to move the ball? Because _____.

  A. ten yards is a long way

  B. eleven men on the other team try to stop the the man with ball

  C. the playing field is very large

  D. eleven men have to catch the ball one by one

(　　)49. If they _____, the teams will play on January 1.

  A. receive six points   B. play eleven games in the season

  C. are the best teams   D. move the ball to the end of the field

(　　)50. Many people come to watch football and they want their team to win. Which of the following is not their act(行为/动作)?

  A. Jumping   B. Dancing   C. Crying   D. Shouting

C

My friend, Hugh, has always been fat, but things got so bad recently that he decided to <u>go on a diet</u>. He began his diet a week ago. First of all, he wrote out a long list of all the foods which were forbidden. The list included most of the things Hugh loves: butter, potatoes, rice, beer, milk, chocolate, and sweets. Yesterday I paid him a visit. I rang the bell and was not surprised to see that Hugh was still as fat as ever. He led me into his room and hurriedly hid a large parcel(包裹) under his desk. It was obvious that he was very embarrassed(尴尬的) when I asked him what he was doing, he smiled guiltily and then put the parcel on the desk. He explained that his diet was so strict that he had to reward (奖励) himself occasionally. Then he showed me the contents of the parcel. It contained five large bars of chocolate and three bags of sweets!

(　　)51. What does the underlined phrase "go on a diet" mean in the passage?
　　　　　A. 饮食。　　　B. 节食。　　　C. 增肥。　　　D. 绝食。

(　　)52. Which was NOT included in Hugh's list when he went on a diet?
　　　　　A. Butter.　　　B. Chocolate.　　　C. Potatoes.　　　D. Tomatoes.

(　　)53. What did Hugh hide under the desk when the writer visited him yesterday?
　　　　　A. A bag.　　　B. A parcel.　　　C. A box.　　　D. A bottle.

(　　)54. Why did Hugh reward himself occasionally according to his own explanation?
　　　　　A. Because his diet was strict.　　　B. Because his diet was not strict.
　　　　　C. Because he was embarrassed.　　　D. Because he was ill.

(　　)55. Did Hugh succeed in his diet?
　　　　　A. Yes, he lost his weight.　　　B. No, he was as fat as ever.
　　　　　C. Yes, he was thinner than ever.　　　D. No, he was much fatter than before.

第二节　词义搭配:从(B)栏中选出(A)栏单词的正确解释。(共10分,每小题1分)

　　　　(A)　　　　　　　　　　　(B)

(　　)56. energetic　　　　A. present

(　　)57. handmade　　　　B. made by a person using their hands

(　　)58. gift　　　　　　　C. little dog

(　　)59. puppy　　　　　　D. severe and must be obeyed completely

(　　)60. strict　　　　　　E. active or strong

(　　)61. visit　　　　　　F. university

(　　)62. college　　　　　G. call on somebody; call at some place

(　　)63. notice　　　　　　H. picture recorded by a camera

(　　)64. photo　　　　　　I. bring something new to

(　　)65. introduce　　　　J. observe or see

第三节　补全对话:根据对话内容,从对话后的选项中选出能填入空白处的最佳选项。(共10分,每小题2分)

A: Excuse me, can you do me a favor?

B: Yes, of course. ___66___

A: ___67___

B: When and where did you last use it?

A: I made a call to my friend when I left my room for lunch, and then I came back to find it lost.

B：___68___

A：OK. I hope it will be found quickly. You know, I'm really worried about it.

B：___69___ Once we get the news, we'll inform you as soon as possible. Please don't worry.

___70___

A：Yes. George, Room 222, sorry to trouble you.

B：You're welcome.

> A. I'll call the Lost and Found Department immediately.
> B. May I have your name and room number?
> C. What's the matter with you, sir?
> D. All right. We'll try our best to find it.
> E. I can't find my mobile phone.

第三部分　语言技能运用(共分四节,满分30分)

第一节　单词拼写:根据下列句子及所给汉语注释,在答题卡上相应题号后的横线上写出该单词的正确形式。(共5分,每小题1分)

71. Welcome to the _____ (职业的) high school.

72. Last month, we _____ (参观) the Great Wall.

73. We all like my mother's _____ (cook).

74. Children like eating junk food, _____ (尤其,特别) fried chicken.

75. Christmas is one of the major _____ (节日) in the United States of America.

第二节　词形变换:用括号内单词的适当形式填空,将正确答案写在答题卡上相应题号后的横线上。(共5分,每小题1分)

76. They are _____ (prepare) a handmade gift for the teacher.

77. Children in English _____ (speak) countries may be named after their parents.

78. I think the Great Wall is worth _____ (visit).

79. He spent over 41 years _____ (travel) throughout the world.

80. In his youth, he was _____ (interest) in geography.

第三节　改错:从A、B、C、D四个画线处找出一处错误的选项,填入答题卡上相应题号后的括号内,并在横线上写出正确答案。(共10分,每小题2分)

81. Why <u>don't</u> you <u>to ask</u> your friends <u>to give</u> you <u>a hand</u>?
　　　　A　　　　B　　　　　　　　C　　　　　D

82. It is <u>easier</u> to <u>say</u> <u>than</u> <u>doing</u>.
　　　A　　　B　　C　　D

83. Ella <u>doesn't</u> <u>does</u> <u>her</u> homework <u>after</u> school.
　　　　A　　　B　　C　　　　　D

84. What time do Bob go swimming every week?
　　　　A　　　B　　　C　　　D
85. My dog runs fast, does he?
　　A　　　B　　C　　D

第四节　书面表达。(共 10 分)

作文题目：My Family

词数要求：80~100 词

写作要点：1. 介绍你的家庭成员；

　　　　　2. 他们的职业、爱好等。

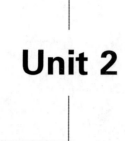

Unit 2

Transportation

Warming up

一、句型汇总

1. I'm going to the Summer Palace. 我要去颐和园。

2. The bus number is right, but you're going in the wrong direction. 公交车号是对的,可是您坐错方向了。

3. You'd better try the subway. 您最好试试坐地铁。

4. There's a station near the next bus stop. 下一个公交车站附近有一个(地铁)站。

5. How long will it take by subway? 坐地铁要多长时间?

6. By the way, it's much greener than taking a taxi. 顺便说一下,这比坐出租车环保多了。

7. And it will be fast and convenient. 而且坐地铁又快又方便。

8. How can I get to the hotel from the airport? 我如何从机场前往酒店?

9. Start from Terminal 1 station, Airport Express Line, change for Subway Line 2 at Zhuquemen station, get off at Zhonghua Square station and take Exit B. 从机场快线1号航站楼站出发,在朱雀门站换乘地铁2号线,至中华广场站下车,从B出口出站。

10. It takes at least one hour, and costs about 80 yuan. 至少需要1个小时,费用约为80元。

二、英汉互译

1. address _____   2. direction _____

3. hire _____

4. province _____

5. bus stop _____

6. 游客_____

7. 方便的_____

8. 机场_____

9. 下车_____

10. 高峰期_____

Listening and Speaking

一、找出与所给单词画线部分读音相同的选项

(　　) 1. <u>a</u>ddress　　A. th<u>a</u>nk　　B. wom<u>a</u>n　　C. <u>a</u>dvice　　D. <u>a</u>ble

(　　) 2. s<u>u</u>bway　　A. h<u>u</u>ge　　B. b<u>u</u>t　　C. <u>u</u>niversity　　D. p<u>u</u>ll

(　　) 3. n<u>ea</u>r　　A. h<u>ea</u>r　　B. h<u>ea</u>rt　　C. s<u>ea</u>rch　　D. b<u>ea</u>r

(　　) 4. h<u>i</u>re　　A. un<u>i</u>t　　B. v<u>i</u>sit　　C. d<u>i</u>strict　　D. l<u>i</u>ke

(　　) 5. <u>ex</u>press　　A. <u>ex</u>ample　　B. <u>ex</u>it　　C. <u>ex</u>pression　　D. <u>ex</u>ercise

二、从B栏中找出与A栏中相对应的答语

　　　　A　　　　　　　　　　　　　　B

A	B
1. Where is the bookstore? 2. You'd better go to bed early today. 3. What's wrong with your sister? 4. Could you tell me the way to the cinema? 5. How do you study English?	A. OK, I will. B. Sure. Go along this street until you reach the first lights. C. She has a fever. D. By making word cards. E. It's next to the cinema.

三、用所给句子补全下面对话

(Li Hua met a foreigner on his way home. "L" is for Li Hua; "F" is for the foreigner.)

F：Excuse me. I'm afraid I am lost. ___1___

L：Sure! Let me see…You're now here near the bus station the heart of the city.

F：Oh…yes. ___2___

L：Go straight down, and then turn left, go straight, and at the third crossing you'll see it on your right.

F：___3___

L：About thirty minutes' walk, and you can also take the No. 1 Bus from this bus station and go 5 stops. You need to get off at People's Park, Renming Gongyuan in Chinese. 4

F：Okay…Thank you!

L：No problem…And, you can also ride a shared bike. Do you have AliPay on your phone? 5

F：Thanks a lot.

L：You're welcome.

> A. How long will it take to walk there?
> B. If you do, you can go there on the bike.
> C. Could you tell me where I am?
> D. Well, how can I get to the nearest bookstore from here?
> E. Ten minutes is enough, if the traffic is good.

四、场景模拟

国外交流生李华在学校门口迷路了,向你询问去学校图书馆的路。请以此为背景编写一组对话。

提示词汇：Excuse me, could you tell me how to get to…?

go along　　turn left　　turn right

at the first crossing

_____

_____

_____

_____

_____

_____

Reading and Writing

一、用括号内所给汉语提示或单词的适当形式填空

1. What's her _____(地址)?

2. We arrived at the _____ (机场) one hour early.

3. Please come whenever it is _____ (方便的) to you.

4. We can find him in this _____ (方向).

5. Which _____ (区) do you live in?

6. He is from Hebei _____ (省) too.

7. I go to school by _____ (地铁).

8. His father is a _____ (出租车) driver.

9. Keep the rules for the public. Be a polite _____ (visit).

10. The weather is very _____ (change) at this time of year.

二、完形填空

A very rich man, Tom, bought a big farm. He spent a lot of money buying it because there was a great __1__ on the farm. People said that the tree was about __2__ hundred years old, and it was famous. __3__ many of his men didn't believe that the tree was so old.

Tom heard that Zeke, one of his men, was very __4__, so he called him to try to make sure how old the tree really was. Four days __5__, Zeke came to Tom and told him that the tree was __6__ than they thought. It was 332 years old.

"Great! How clever you are!" said Tom. "But I want to know __7__ you could tell the tree was so old."

"Very __8__! I cut down the tree and counted the rings," answered Zeke __9__.

Tom stood there, saying __10__ more.

( ) 1. A. river   B. tree   C. rock   D. building
( ) 2. A. three   B. four   C. five   D. six
( ) 3. A. And   B. So   C. Or   D. But
( ) 4. A. strong   B. kind   C. clever   D. happy
( ) 5. A. after   B. ago   C. later   D. before
( ) 6. A. older   B. larger   C. lighter   D. heavier
( ) 7. A. when   B. where   C. how   D. why
( ) 8. A. easy   B. difficult   C. hard   D. lucky
( ) 9. A. sadly   B. proudly   C. luckily   D. hardly
( ) 10. A. something   B. nothing   C. anything   D. everything

三、阅读理解

阅读下面短文，从每题所给的 A、B、C、D 四个选项中选出最佳答案。

45 students are in our class. I made a survey(调查). 6 students say they like to exercise. Most boys play basketball together twice a week. But girls think basketball is difficult for them, they like to play volleyball together twice a week.

My friend, Tony, is good at running. He runs for 30 minutes on the playground every evening before he goes to bed. Is it interesting? Gray is good at swimming. He goes to the swimming club three times a month in winter, and three times a week in summer. So he is pretty healthy.

Some of my classmates have good eating habits. They eat both meat and vegetables. 60% of them drink milk every day. 15 students say they drink milk three or four times a week. But some students like to eat junk food, especially Sally. What's worse(更糟糕的) is that she doesn't like to exercise, so she is very fat. "I want to lose weight(减肥) tomorrow," she always says.

(   )1. How often do most boys play basketball?

  A. Every day.   B. Twice a day.

  C. Twice a week.   D. Three times a week.

(   )2. Why do the girls dislike playing basketball?

  A. Because they have no time.

  B. Because they think it is not easy.

  C. Because they don't like to play with the boys.

  D. Because they are not strong enough.

(   )3. When does Tony often run for 30 minutes?

  A. Every afternoon.

  B. Every morning.

  C. Every evening before he goes to bed.

  D. Every noon.

(   )4. How often does Gray swim in winter?

  A. Three times a month.   B. Three times a week.

  C. Hardly ever.   D. Once a month.

(   )5. Why is Sally so fat?

  A. Because she doesn't like to exercise.

  B. Because she likes to eat junk food very much.

  C. Because she doesn't like to exercise, and she likes to eat junk food.

  D. Because her families are fat.

四、书面表达

请写一篇文章分析日常几种交通工具的优缺点(80~100词)。

_____
_____
_____
_____
_____
_____
_____

Grammar

一、从下面每小题四个选项中选出最佳选项

(   ) 1. Don't _____ afraid of speaking in front of the whole class!
      A. /   B. be   C. is   D. to be

(   ) 2. —_____ late for class again! —Sorry, I won't.
      A. Don't   B. Can't   C. Don't be   D. Doesn't arrive

(   ) 3. _____ you close the door when you leave the room.
      A. Make sure   B. Making sure   C. To make sure   D. Makes sure

(   ) 4. _____ soccer in the street. It's too dangerous.
      A. Not play   B. No play   C. Don't play   D. Not to play

(   ) 5. _____ get off the bus until it stops.
      A. Can't   B. Don't   C. Aren't   D. Doesn't

(   ) 6. Let's _____ the monkeys first. They are very smart.
      A. see   B. to see   C. watches   D. to watch

(   ) 7. —_____ bring mobile phone to school, Bob!
    —Sorry, Mr. Smith. I _____ do that again.
      A. Not; don't   B. Don't; am not   C. Don't; won't   D. Not; don't

(   ) 8. _____ any noise in class.
      A. Not make   B. Don't make   C. Not to make   D. Makes

(   ) 9. —Look at the sign there, what does it mean?
    —Don't _____ swimming, it's dangerous.
      A. going   B. went   C. go   D. goes

(   ) 10. Now students, _____ your plans for the coming year.

A. writing down   B. write down   C. to write down   D. wrote down

( )11. Please _____ quiet, Tony. Your mother _____ now.
A. be; is sleeping   B. being; is sleeping
C. be; sleeping   D. being; sleeping

( )12. Hurry up, _____ you'll miss the train.
A. but   B. so   C. and   D. or

( )13. Sit down and _____ some water, please.
A. to drink   B. drinking   C. drink   D. drinks

( )14. —Peter, _____ talking. You must be quiet in the library.
—Sorry, Miss Wang.
A. stop to   B. stop   C. stops   D. stopped

( )15. _____ me a chance and I'll bring you a surprise.
A. Give   B. Giving   C. Gives   D. To give

( )16. —Let's _____ volleyball this afternoon.
—Sorry, I want _____ my uncle.
A. to play; to meet   B. to play; meeting
C. play; to meet   D. play; meet

( )17. Dear me! Just _____ at the time! I _____ no idea it was so late.
A. look; have   B. looking; had   C. look; had   D. looking; have

( )18. Life is like a journey. _____ ahead, and you will see a lot more beautiful sceneries(风景).
A. Plan   B. To plan   C. Planning   D. Plans

( )19. _____ throwing those stones, please.
A. Stop   B. Stops   C. Stopping   D. Stopped

( )20. —_____ up, Anna. It's seven thirty.
—One more minute, mother.
A. To get   B. Get   C. Getting   D. Gets

( )21. —Dave, _____ to clean the living room.
—OK, I will do it now.
A. don't forget   B. don't remember   C. forget not   D. remember not

( )22. —Boys and girls, welcome to my home and _____.
—Thank you.
A. help yourselves   B. help yourself
C. help you   D. to help yourselves

(　　)23. Let's go and _____ his new shoes.

　　　　A. see　　　　B. to see　　　　C. seeing　　　　D. sees

(　　)24. _____ go to bed too late, Jack. You have to get up early tomorrow morning.

　　　　A. Don't　　　B. Doesn't　　　C. Didn't　　　D. hadn't

(　　)25. —_____ the milk, Peter! It's good for your health.

　　　　—OK, Mom.

　　　　A. Drinks　　　B. Drinking　　　C. Drink　　　D. To drink

(　　)26. —How can I get to the post office?

　　　　—_____ the bridge and you'll see it on your left.

　　　　A. Go cross　　　B. Go across　　　C. Go crossing　　　D. Across

(　　)27. —Excuse me, can you tell me the way to the museum?

　　　　—_____ along the road, and turn left _____ the second turning, the museum is beside the post station.

　　　　A. To walk; on　　B. Walking; on　　C. Walk; at　　D. To walking; at

(　　)28. Don't _____ in class. The teacher will be angry(生气).

　　　　A. listen music　　　　　　　　B. to listen to music

　　　　C. listen to music　　　　　　　D. to listen music

(　　)29. —_____ the books in the bookcase, Jerry.

　　　　—OK.

　　　　A. Put　　　B. To put　　　C. Putting　　　D. Puts

(　　)30. —Tom, _____ the umbrella(雨伞) with you. It's going to rain.

　　　　—OK, Mom.

　　　　A. taking　　　B. takes　　　C. take　　　D. is taking

二、找出下列句子中错误的选项，并改正过来

1. Doesn't play with fire because it's very dangerous.
　　A　　　　B　　　C　　　D

2. Worked hard and you'll make progress in English.
　　A　　　B　　C　　　　　　　D

3. Mom, don't worried about me.
　　A　　B　　　C　　D

4. Please help me carry it, shall we?
　　　　A　　B　　　C　　D

5. Don't make so much noise, do you?
　　A　　　　B　　　C　　　D

6. Tell me the truth, and I'll be angry.
　　A　　　B　　　C　　　D

7. Kate, brings your homework here tomorrow.
         A   B   C   D

8. Walking along this street, and you can find the hotel on your right.
   A   B   C   D

9. Please to read it again more slowly.
      A   B   C   D

10. Please not sit next to Nancy.
      A   B   C   D

For Better Performance

一、找出与所给单词画线部分读音相同的选项

(   ) 1. province   A. most   B. lose   C. note   D. problem
(   ) 2. direction   A. especially B. these   C. less   D. the
(   ) 3. taxi   A. attract   B. animal   C. advice   D. address
(   ) 4. airport   A. afford   B. visitor   C. worth   D. world
(   ) 5. district   A. high   B. life   C. kite   D. tip

二、英汉互译

1. change _____   2. district _____
3. express _____   4. subway _____
5. terminal _____   6. 班车 _____
7. 担心 _____   8. 最好 _____
9. 到达 _____   10. 乘出租车 _____

三、用括号内所给汉语提示或单词的适当形式填空

1. There are many _____ (游客) in Beijing every year.
2. The 8:00 a.m. _____ (快线) is crowded.
3. The second _____ (航站楼) is opened in 1998.
4. _____ (换乘) for line 2 at the next station.
5. We _____ (租用) a car yesterday.
6. He will paint the gate _____ (绿色的).
7. I will meet you at the main _____ (enter).
8. Turn left at the first _____ (turn).

9. From now on I will be more _____ (care).
10. You will be quite _____ (comfort) here.

四、找出下列句子中错误的选项,并改正过来

1. How long will it take in subway?
      A   B C D

2. You had better to drive slowly and carefully.
        A   B   C   D

3. He is going on the wrong direction.
      A   B   C   D

4. That took me two hours to finish my homework.
      A B   C   D

5. I had to wait half a hour for a bus.
     A   B   C   D

单元检测

第一部分　英语知识运用(共分三节,满分40分)

第一节　语音知识:从 A、B、C、D 四个选项中找出其画线部分与所给单词画线部分读音相同的选项。(共5分,每小题1分)

(　　) 1. worry　　A. try　　　　B. fly　　　　C. happy　　　D. supply

(　　) 2. change　A. technology　B. stomach　　C. Christmas　D. children

(　　) 3. direction　A. which　　B. light　　　C. kite　　　　D. website

(　　) 4. rush　　　A. unit　　　B. university　C. bus　　　　D. useful

(　　) 5. hour　　　A. honest　　B. hard　　　C. his　　　　D. human

第二节　词汇与语法知识:从 A、B、C、D 四个选项中选出可以填入空白处的最佳选项。(共25分,每小题1分)

(　　) 6. You can easily find a taxi here. The transportation in our city is very _____.
    A. convenient　　B. cheap　　　C. crowded　　D. quick

(　　) 7. Don't _____. We'll soon solve this problem.
    A. worry　　　　B. mind　　　　C. speak　　　D. return

(　　) 8. If you look at your map, you'll see the _____ Center at the bottom. Let's go there to buy the tickets.
    A. Kitchen　　　B. Community　C. Company　　D. Visitor

(   ) 9. _____ your hands before dinner, Tony.
   A. Washes   B. Washing   C. To wash   D. Wash

(   ) 10. Go _____ this road for three minutes and you will see the supermarket.
   A. off   B. on   C. along   D. right

(   ) 11. The sign "_____" means that people can't smoke here.
   A. Don't Smoking   B. No Smoking   C. No Smoke   D. Not Smoke

(   ) 12. I tell my mother not _____ me.
   A. worry about   B. to worry   C. to worry about   D. worry

(   ) 13. —Mum, can I do the homework tomorrow?
   —You _____ finish it today.
   A. had better   B. had rather
   C. had better don't   D. had rather not

(   ) 14. It _____ about two hours _____ their homework every day.
   A. costs; to do   B. spends; doing
   C. takes; doing   D. takes; to do

(   ) 15. —_____ can I keep these fashion magazines?
   —About half a month.
   A. How far   B. How long   C. How often   D. How soon

(   ) 16. My brother usually goes to school _____.
   A. by bus   B. in bus   C. on bus   D. take a bus

(   ) 17. We can _____ to school.
   A. by bus   B. take bus   C. take a bus   D. have a bus

(   ) 18. I often go to school _____.
   A. by a bus   B. in a bus   C. take a bus   D. on a bus

(   ) 19. She plays basketball for _____ every day.
   A. half an hour   B. a half hour   C. an half hour   D. half hour

(   ) 20. —_____ does Tony go to school?
   —He goes to school by bus.
   A. How   B. What   C. When   D. Why

(   ) 21. _____ wake up your sister, Ben. She needs a good sleep.
   A. Don't   B. Doesn't   C. Aren't   D. Can't

(   ) 22. _____ a job you love, and you'll never work a day in your life.
   A. Find   B. Finding   C. to find   D. Found

(   ) 23. Please _____ look outside. Look at the blackboard.

    A. not   B. don't   C. aren't   D. can't

( )24. —When do you usually _____ school?

    —At about 8 a.m.

    A. come   B. arrive   C. reach to   D. get to

( )25. Here comes the bus. You'd better _____.

    A. get on it   B. get it off   C. to get on it   D. to get it off

( )26. _____ get off the bus _____ it stops.

    A. Please, until B. Don't, after C. Please, before D. Don't, until

( )27. Put on your warm clothes before you go out, _____ you may have a cold.

    A. or   B. so   C. but   D. and

( )28. Hold on to your dreams _____ one day they may just come true.

    A. so   B. but   C. and   D. or

( )29. — Where is Mary?

    — She is waiting for the bus _____ the bus stop.

    A. of   B. at   C. on   D. to

( )30. —Thank you for your help.

    —_____.

    A. No problem   B. That's great

    C. The same to you   D. Yes, please

第三节 完形填空:阅读下面的短文,从所给的 A、B、C、D 四个选项中选出正确的答案。(共 10 分,每小题 1 分)

Everyone wants to have healthy teeth.

When you laugh, you will __31__ your mouth and show your teeth. Your teeth are important __32__ many ways. Take care of them, and they'll help to take care of you. Strong __33__ teeth help you grow. They also help you speak clearly. You can take care of your teeth by doing like these:

Brush your teeth __34__ a day, after getting up and before bedtime. And you should brush __35__ of your teeth, not just the front ones. Spend some time on the teeth along the sides and in the back. Take your time while brushing. Spend __36__ than three minutes each time you brush. Ask your parents to help you get a new toothbrush __37__ three months. Clean __38__ your teeth with dental floss(牙线). Brushing __39__ your teeth healthy. You also need to care about what you eat and drink. Eat more fruits and vegetables and drink __40__.

Do you want to have white and healthy teeth? Please brush your teeth!

( )31. A. open   B. wash   C. serve   D. close

(	)32. A. by	B. on	C. for	D. in
(	)33. A. happy	B. white	C. healthy	D. clean
(	)34. A. once	B. twice	C. three times	D. four times
(	)35. A. one	B. some	C. all	D. most
(	)36. A. less	B. more	C. better	D. fewer
(	)37. A. both	B. every	C. for	D. too
(	)38. A. and	B. with	C. between	D. on
(	)39. A. keeps	B. produces	C. starts	D. suggests
(	)40. A. water	B. juice	C. coffee	D. cola

第二部分　篇章与词汇理解(共分三节　满分 50 分)

第一节　阅读理解:阅读下列短文,从每题所给的 A、B、C、D 四个选项中,选出最恰当的答案。(共 30 分,每小题 2 分)

A

Many people die or are seriously injured on the roads in our country each year. As a driver, how can you avoid traffic accidents? Here are some tips for you.

First, never drive too fast, as speeding is a major factor in many accidents.

Second, always keep your vehicle in good condition and replace the worn parts in time.

Third, remember to fasten your seat belt. It will protect you if the car stops or changes direction suddenly. It is very dangerous to drive without a seat belt on.

Fourth, keep a safe distance from other vehicles!

Fifth, watch the traffic lights and other vehicles carefully as many accidents are easy to happen at the crossing.

Sixth, reading, drinking, eating, smoking, or talking on the phone while driving can be very dangerous, because you need two hands to drive a car!

Finally, never drink wine or beer before driving!

Please take care while driving so that you can arrive safely.

Happy driving!

( )41. Which is the main cause of traffic accidents?
　　A. Vehicle in bad condition.　　B. Driving too fast.
　　C. Reading while driving.　　D. Drinking wine before driving.

( )42. What should we do if we want to keep the car in good condition?
　　A. Keep a safe distance.　　B. Watch the traffic lights.
　　C. Replace the worn parts in time.　　D. Drive carefully.

(　　)43. In which case, fasten seat belt will protect you?

　　A. When the car turn around the corner.

　　B. When the car runs in a fast speed.

　　C. When the car is too close to the car in front of you.

　　D. When the car stops or changes direction suddenly.

(　　)44. All of the behaviors below are unsafe while driving except _____.

　　A. listening to the radio　　B. reading

　　C. smoking　　D. talking on the phone

(　　)45. What's the best title for this passage?

　　A. How to solve driving problems.　　B. How to avoid traffic accidents.

　　C. How to learn traffic rules.　　D. How to get driving skills.

B

　　It's our duty to protect our environment. People all over the world have come up with good ideas. In Britain, a popular shopping bag has been used by some of the world's most beautiful women. Its official price is £ 5, but as much as £ 400 online. The bag's name is "I'm Not a Plastic Bag". It is made of cotton. It is so "hot" that everyone wants to get one. Supporters see fashion as a way to move away from the plastic bags. In this way, not so many plastic bags will be given by supermarkets.

　　When the bags were first sold, nearly 500 people waited in line to buy one. So far, about 20,000 of the popular bags have been sold at school largest supermarket. Supporters think it is one of the ways to encourage shoppers to use the reusable bags instead of the plastic ones. The bag has also become a "must-have" for many famous people, just because they want to be fashionable and at the same time care about the environment.

　　The designer of the bag has been asked to design a kind of bags by the "We Are What We Do" group. The group believes that each person in Great Britain uses about 167 plastic bags a year and that small lifestyle changes can have a strong effect on reducing waste and protecting environment. It also believes that everyone should try his best to protect the earth from being polluted. Only in this way can our planet become more beautiful.

(　　)46. Where can we buy the popular bags?

　　A. In America.　　B. In China.　　C. In Germany.　　D. In Britain.

(　　)47. We can use "_____" to describe the bag.

　　A. Green　　B. Colorful　　C. Common　　D. Expensive

(　　)48. Which of the following is TRUE?

　　A. The popular bags sell at an official price of £ 5 online.

B. So far, the popular bags have been sold at all the supermarkets in Great Britain.

C. Small lifestyle changes can have a strong effect on reducing waste and the environmental pollution.

D. "We Are What We Do" group means a business that sells bags.

( )49. What's the purpose of designing the popular bags?

A. To make money.

B. To help famous people.

C. To reduce the environmental pollution.

D. To make women fashionable.

( )50. From the passage, we can know _____

A. the designer has been asked to develop the bag.

B. it's everyone's duty to produce popular bags.

C. each person can use about 167 plastic bags every year.

D. it's everyone's duty to protect the environment and produce less pollution.

C

Many teenagers feel that the most important people in their lives are their friends. They believe that their family members don't know as well as their friends do. In large families, it is quite often for brothers and sisters to fight with each other and then they can only go to their friends for some ideas.

It is very important for teenagers to have some good friends. Even when they are not with their friends, they usually spend a lot of time talking among themselves on the phone. This communication(交际) is very important in children's growing up, because friends can discuss something. These things are difficult to say to their family members.

However, parents often try to choose their children's friends for them. Some parents may even stop their children from meeting their friends.

Have you ever thought of the following questions?

Who choose your friends?

Do you choose your friends or your friends choose you?

Have you got a good friend your parents don't like? Your answers are welcome.

( )51. Many teenagers think that _____ can understand them better.

A. friends   B. brothers   C. sisters   D. parents

( )52. _____ is very important to teenagers.

A. To make friends   B. Communication

C. To stop meeting friends   D. Both A and B

( )53. When teenagers have something difficult to say to their parents, they usually _____.

  A. stay alone at home

  B. fight with their friends

  C. discuss it with their friends

  D. go to their brothers or sisters for help

( )54. The sentence "Your answers are welcome." means "_____".

  A. You are welcome to discuss the questions with us

  B. We have no idea, so your answers are welcome

  C. Your answers are always right

  D. You can give us all the right answers

( )55. Which of the following is the writer's attitude(态度)?

  A. Parents should choose friends for their children.

  B. Children should choose everything they like.

  C. Parents should understand their children.

  D. Teenagers should only go to their friends for help.

第二节　词义搭配:从(B)栏中选出(A)栏单词的正确解释。(共10分,每小题1分)

(A)	(B)
( )56. address	A. pay money to borrow sth. for a short time
( )57. convenient	B. a person who is traveling in a car, bus, train, etc
( )58. hire	C. a door or passage used for entering a place
( )59. green	D. having the color of grass
( )60. near	E. useful, easy or quick to do
( )61. province	F. a person who visits a person or place
( )62. subway	G. a short distance away
( )63. visitor	H. an underground railway
( )64. passenger	I. details of where sb lives or works
( )65. entrance	J. one of the areas that some countries are divided into with its own government

第三节　补全对话:根据对话内容,从对话后的选项中选出能填入空白处的最佳选项。(共10分,每小题2分)

Ella Baker: Good morning, I'm Ella Baker, a new student here.

Lin Yang: Good morning! 66

Ella Baker: I need to go to the library. 67

Lin Yang: Of course. Keep going in this direction and turn left at Teaching Building 1. Then go along the road and turn right. ___68___ Then you will see the library on your left.

Ella Baker: Keep going and turn left at…you lost me there.

Lin Yang: ___69___

Ella Baker: Really? ___70___

> A. Turn left again at the first turning.
> B. Why don't we go there together?
> C. I'm Lin Yang from IT class, grade 1.
> D. That's very kind of you!
> E. Can you tell me where it is?

第三部分　语言技能运用(共分四节　满分30分)

第一节　单词拼写:根据下列句子及所给汉语注释,在答题卡上相应题号后的横线上写出该单词的正确形式。(共5分,每小题1分)

71. There is a park _____ (临近) my school.

72. Where is the _____ (出口).

73. I sat in the _____ (乘客) seat.

74. The company was clearly at the _____ (十字路口).

75. She was wearing an _____ (昂贵的) new coat.

第二节　词形变换:用括号内单词的适当形式填空,将正确答案写在答题卡上相应题号后的横线上。(共5分,每小题1分)

76. He is _____ (worry) about the maths exam.

77. Riding a bike is _____ (green) than taking a taxi.

78. Be _____ (care) with the wet floor.

79. We live in _____ (north) China.

80. We have _____ (differ) likes and dislikes.

第三节　改错:从 A、B、C、D 四个画线处找出一处错误的选项填入答题卡上相应题号后的括号内,并在横线上写出正确答案。(共10分,每小题2分)

81. She <u>rushed</u> to <u>get</u> the post office <u>before</u> it <u>closed</u>.
       A   B   C   D

82. <u>In</u> the <u>way</u>, <u>when</u> is the <u>final</u> exam?
     A   B   C   D

83. <u>Don't</u> <u>worry</u> <u>at</u> <u>me</u>.
       A   B   C D

84. That took me half an hour to go to school.
    ‾A   ‾B   ‾C   ‾D

85. Then you will find the library in your left.
             ‾A   ‾B   ‾C ‾D

第四节　书面表达。(共 10 分)

作文题目:The Way of Going to School

词数要求:80~100 词

写作要点:介绍现如今学生上学的交通方式以及它们的优缺点。

Unit 3

Shopping

Warming up

一、句型汇总

1. Where do you usually buy these things? 你通常在哪儿买这些东西?

2. What is this in English? 这个用英语怎么说? It's a pair of jeans. 它是一条牛仔裤。

3. How can I help you? /Can I help you? / What can I do for you? 要我帮忙吗?

4. I'd like a pair of jeans. 我想买一条牛仔裤。

5. What color is it? 它是什么颜色的? It is red. 它是红色的。

6. What is it made of/from? 它是用什么制成的? It is made of cotton. 它是用棉花制成的。

7. What size is it? 它是多大尺码的? It is a medium one. 它是中号的。(It is size S/L/XL/XXL.)

8. The fitting room is over there. 试衣间在那边。

9. I think they are a bit tight, do you have a larger size? 它有点紧,有大一点的吗?

10. How much is it? 多少钱? It is 150 yuan. 150 元。

11. I will take it. 我买了。

12. Can I pay with my cell phone? 我可以用手机支付吗?
Sure. Please show me your payment code. 请出示你的付款码。
Here you are. 给你。

13. The Internet is changing the way we shop. 互联网正在改变着我们的购物方式。

In recent years, more and more people choose to go shopping on the Internet. 近几年,越来越多的人选择在网上购物。

14. To encourage online shopping, some online stores offer huge discount on special days of the year. 为了鼓励网上购物,有些网上店铺在一些特殊的日子会提供巨大的折扣。

One of them is the Black Friday shopping day. 其中一个就是黑色星期五购物节。

二、英汉互译

1. communication _____   2. compare with _____
3. fit for _____   4. 给……提供_____
5. 引向_____   6. 打折销售_____
7. pay with _____   8. 商店店员_____
9. 支付码_____   10. material _____
11. 传统的_____   12. 原来的_____

Listening and Speaking

一、找出与所给单词画线部分读音相同的选项

(   )1. <u>a</u>dd   A. <u>a</u>sk   B. t<u>a</u>ke   C. <u>a</u>pple   D. <u>a</u>gree

(   )2. <u>c</u>ompare   A. <u>c</u>ommunication   B. <u>c</u>ome   C. <u>c</u>otton   D. <u>c</u>ode

(   )3. en<u>ou</u>gh   A. ab<u>ou</u>t   B. tr<u>ou</u>ble   C. disc<u>ou</u>nt   D. m<u>ou</u>ntain

(   )4. ques<u>tion</u>   A. edi<u>tion</u>   B. communica<u>tion</u> C. sugges<u>tion</u> D. tradi<u>tion</u>al

(   )5. f<u>ea</u>ture   A. br<u>ea</u>d   B. l<u>ea</u>d   C. br<u>ea</u>kfast   D. sw<u>ea</u>ter

二、从B栏中找出与A栏中相对应的答语

A	B
1. What is this in English? 2. What can I do for you? 3. Can I try it on? 4. How much are they? 5. Do you have a larger size?	A. Sure, the fitting room is over there. B. Yes, try this pair please. C. They are 100 yuan in total. D. I'd like a pair of jeans. E. It is a sweater.

三、用所给句子补全下面对话

A：Do you know what is shopping online?

B：Yes. __1__

A：Really? Could you tell me some advantages of it?

B：Of course. Firstly, __2__ You can buy anything you want and they will send it to your home or any place you want.

A：Wow, that is great.

B：Yes. What's more. __3__

A：Ah, that is quite a smart way for shopping. What is its disadvantages do you think?

B：Well, __4__ I can only look at the pictures and some introduction of it. You can not try it on if you buy some clothes or shoes. Sometimes you may get the one not fit you from the Internet.

A：I agree with you. __5__

B：You can return them if you are not satisfied now. Thus, I think shopping online will be a trend in this age. It plays a more and more important role in our daily life.

A：Thanks a lot for your introduction. It helps a lot!

B：You are welcome.

> A. How to deal with this?
> B. It is much cheaper than the goods in big shopping mall.
> C. I bought a lot of things from the Internet.
> D. it is very convenient.
> E. the biggest one is that I cannot see the true goods.

四、场景模拟

编一组对话：和妈妈一起去商场买衣服。

提示词组：Can I help you ? /What can I do for you? I'd like to buy…

Do you have some light green ones?　　I want to try them on.

Is credit card available? （可以用信用卡吗？）It's too expensive for me/It's cheap.

How much are they?　　I'll take them.

Unit 3   Shopping

Reading and Writing

一、用括号内所给汉语提示或单词的适当形式填空

1. Through the Internet we can _____ (communication) with the people from far away.

2. When they got to the hotel, they tied the horse to the tree _____ (tight).

3. If you come to China on the Spring Festival, you can learn more about China's _____ (tradition) culture.

4. In winter, I like wearing the clothes _____ (make) of fur(毛皮).

5. You'd better go to the _____ (fit) room to try on the coat.

6. _____ (比较) with the old one, the new school looks more like a big garden.

7. If you give me a better _____ (折扣), I will take the two coats.

8. In the shopping mall, you can find the clothes in different _____ (款式,风格).

9. We will _____ (提供,给) you a better discount, if you give us the five-star rating.

10. The things made of good _____ (材质,材料) usually cost more.

二、完形填空

A plane took off, a passenger needed a cup of water to take his medicine. An air hostess told that she would bring him the   1   soon. But the air hostess was   2   busy that she forgot to bring him the water.   3   the passenger couldn't take his medicine on time. About half an hour later, she hurried over to him with a cup of water, but he   4   it.

In the following hours, each time she   5   the passenger, she would ask him with a smile whether he needed help or not. But the passenger   6   paid notice to her.

When it was time to get off the   7 , the passenger asked her to hand him the passengers' booklet(留言簿), she was very   8 . She thought that he would   9   bad words in it, but with a smile she handed it to him.

Off the plane, she opened the booklet and then   10 . The passenger put it, "In the past few hours, you have asked me whether I needed help or not twelve times in all. How can I refuse your twelve faithful smiles?"

(　　) 1. A. medicine   B. water   C. cup   D. coffee
(　　) 2. A. very   B. too   C. quite   D. so
(　　) 3. A. With her help   B. As are result   C. On the one hand   D. To tell the truth

( )4. A. drank   B. accepted   C. refused   D. received
( )5. A. looked at   B. listened to   C. talked about   D. passed by
( )6. A. usually   B. never   C. sometimes   D. often
( )7. A. plane   B. train   C. ship   D. bus
( )8. A. interested   B. happy   C. excited   D. sad
( )9. A. break down   B. get down   C. write down   D. go down
( )10. A. smiled   B. laughed   C. wondered   D. worried

三、阅读理解

阅读下面短文,从每题所给的 A、B、C、D 四个选项中选出最佳答案。

Have you noticed your life becoming a little easier? Now, when you go to a certain shopping mall, you can enjoy its free WiFi there. When you want to take a taxi, you can book one with your phone. In fact, all these can be seen as the basic parts of a smart city.

The idea of a smart city was brought up by US company IBM in 2010. Generally, a smart city is a city that uses modern technologies such as the Internet to improve city planning, save money and resources, and make our life convenient. How smart can a city become? Here are great examples.

In 2009, Dubuque became the first smart city in the US. The city used smart water meters(水表) to take the place of traditional water meters. They can detect(探测) water waste and leakage(泄漏) and send data to let the house owner know. The same system is used for other city resources like electricity and natural gas. By this way, people know how much they have used and are glad to help reduce waste.

Santander in Spain also gives us a look at the future. If people point a cellphone toward a nearby bus stop, the phone can show all the bus lines that serve the stop. The government has also organized a research team and provided an App(应用程序) that collects data on almost everything: light, temperature, and the movements of cars and people. Opening the App near a supermarket, it can provide the immediate information on special offers.

( )1. What makes the life easier than it used to be?
     A. Free Wi-Fi.   B. Smart phones.
     C. Taxies.   D. Modern technologies.

( )2. The underlined word "convenient" is the closest in meaning to _____.
     A. useful   B. normal   C. suitable   D. easy

( )3. Compared to traditional city facilities, smart system do better in _____.
     A. detecting water leakage

B. sending data to the house owners

C. encouraging people to save city resources

D. saving electricity and gas

(　　) 4. The example of Santander shows the use of smart systems in aspects(方面) EXCEPT _____.

A. business　　　　　　　　B. health care

C. traffic controlling　　　D. public transportation

(　　) 5. What's the main idea of the passage?

A. Digital technologies help improve city planning.

B. Smart cities will make our future life better and easier.

C. Smart cities are very common in both Dubuque and Santander.

D. Spain and the US take the leading position in building smart cities.

四、书面表达

作文题目:The Supermarket Nearby

词数要求:80~100 词

写作要点:1. 你经常购物吗?

2. 谈谈你附近的超市。

_____

_____

_____

_____

_____

_____

Grammar

一、从下面每小题四个选项中选出最佳选项

(　　) 1. They have produced _____ steel this year as they did five years ago.

A. twice as much　　B. twice as many　　C. twice more as　　D. as twice much

(　　) 2. His handwriting is _____ than mine.
    A. good　　　　B. better　　　　C. best　　　　D. well

(　　) 3. He swims as _____ as possible in the match.
    A. quick　　　　B. quicker　　　　C. quickly　　　　D. more quickly

(　　) 4. Liu Mei jumped as _____ as Liu Li did in the long jump.
    A. far　　　　B. farther　　　　C. long　　　　D. longer

(　　) 5. This street is much _____ than that one.
    A. straight　　　　B. straighter　　　　C. straightest　　　　D. more straighter

(　　) 6. 8 years old as the boy is, he studies harder than _____.
    A. anyother boys　　　　B. any another boy
    C. anyone else　　　　D. any of other boy

(　　) 7. It's believed that _____ you work _____ result you'd get.
    A. the harder; the better　　　　B. the more hard; the more good
    C. the harder; the good　　　　D. the more hard; the better

(　　) 8. The dress is very beautiful, but it's _____ more expensive than that one.
    A. more　　　　B. very　　　　C. much　　　　D. most

(　　) 9. Last night my father went back _____ later than before.
    A. quite　　　　B. very　　　　C. even　　　　D. much more

(　　) 10. —We should speak English in and after class.
    —Yes, the _____ you speak, the _____ you speak.
    A. more; better　　B. much; good　　C, much; better　　D. often; better

(　　) 11. Which is the _____ country, Japan or Australia?
    A. more developed　　　　B. more developing
    C. most developed　　　　D. most developing

(　　) 12. Our country becomes _____.
    A. stronger and stronger　　　　B. strong and strong
    C. more strong and more strong　　　　D. more and more strong

(　　) 13. This picture is _____ than that one.
    A. more beautiful　　　　B. beautiful
    C. beautifuler　　　　D. the most beautiful

(　　) 14. Of all his outdoor activities, Paul likes fishing _____, but he doesn't enjoy eating fish.
    A. good　　　　B. well　　　　C. better　　　　D. best

Unit 3　Shopping

(　　) 15. Which is _____ book, the new one or the old one?
　　　　A. better　　　　B. the better　　　　C. best　　　　D. the best

(　　) 16. Tom plays tennis very badly, Carl plays even _____.
　　　　A. badlier　　　　B. more badly　　　　C. worse　　　　D. worst

(　　) 17. He drives much _____ than he did 3 years ago.
　　　　A. careful　　　　B. carefully　　　　C. more careful　　　　D. more carefully

(　　) 18. Of all the satellites, the moon is _____ the earth.
　　　　A. the nearest to　　　B. to nearer to　　　C. the nearer to　　　D. nearest to

(　　) 19. I bought _____ meat yesterday as he bought today.
　　　　A. as twice much　　B. as much twice　　C. twice as much　　D. twice much as

(　　) 20. The Yellow River is _____ river in China.
　　　　A. a second longest
　　　　B. the second longer
　　　　C. a second longer
　　　　D. the second longest

(　　) 21. This university is _____ than that one.
　　　　A. 3 times larger　　B. larger 3 times　　C. 3 times large　　D. large 3 times

(　　) 22. My grandfather is _____.
　　　　A. as 3 times old as
　　　　B. 3 times as old as
　　　　C. 3 times as older as
　　　　D. as 3 times older as

(　　) 23. The railway is very convenient and cheap, and the ship becomes _____.
　　　　A. more important　　B. important　　　C. not important　　　D. less important

(　　) 24. She isn't _____ I.
　　　　A. so tall as　　　　B. as tall as　　　　C. so taller as　　　　D. as taller as

(　　) 25. Liu Lei is taller than _____.
　　　　A. any other students
　　　　B. any other student
　　　　C. anyone
　　　　D. else anyone

(　　) 26. The room is _____ of that one.
　　　　A. 3 times long
　　　　B. 3 times the length
　　　　C. 3 times length
　　　　D. the length 3 times

(　　) 27. This building is _____ of that one.
　　　　A. 2 times high
　　　　B. twice height
　　　　C. twice the height
　　　　D. two times the height

(　　) 28. This new coat costs me _____ the last one I bought two years ago.
　　　　A. three times as more as
　　　　B. three times as much as

— 43 —

    C. as three times much as   D. as much as three times

( )29. China is one of _____ in the world.

    A. much older country   B. much older countries

    C. the oldest countries   D. the oldest country

( )30. Of the two toys, John chose _____.

    A. the less expensive one   B. less expensive one

    C. the most expensive   D. the least expensive

二、找出下列句子中错误的选项，并改正过来

( )1. He will come to see me if he will have time tomorrow.
     A B C   D

( )2. I want to do some shopping after I leave Beijing for home.
     A   B C   D

( )3. What do you like this sweater?
    A B C D

( )4. He was made teach the students in another way.
     A B   C D

( )5. I think you want to say it in English, don't I?
    A   B   C   D

( )6. Comparing with the old time, people are living a better life now.
     A   B   C   D

( )7. How about go to see a movie tonight?
     A B   D

( )8. Will you pay in cash or in your cell phone?
     A B C D

( )9. This T-shirt is too small. I need a large size.
    A B   C   D

( )10. John speaks English gooder than Ben does.
     A   B C D

For Better Performance

一、找出与所给单词画线部分读音相同的选项

( )1. re<u>s</u>ource A. convenience B. cotton C. discount D. office

( )2. jean<u>s</u>   A. mean<u>s</u>   B. coat<u>s</u> C. desk<u>s</u> D. sale

( )3. s<u>i</u>lk   A. s<u>i</u>ze   B. onl<u>i</u>ne C. t<u>i</u>ght D. f<u>i</u>tting

( )4. code　　　A. online　　　B. offer　　　C. font　　　D. told

( )5. style　　　A. play　　　B. slowly　　　C. why　　　D. copy

二、英汉互译

1. 节省时间_____　　　2. 在任何时间_____

3. 更低的价格_____　　　4. 有更多的产品供你选择_____

5. 更多关于产品的信息_____　　　6. in English _____

7. both… and…_____　　　8. compare to _____

9. traditional Chinese culture _____　　　10. as…as _____

三、用括号内所给汉语提示或单词的适当形式填空

1. We should remember the China-Japan Wars _____(历史).

2. A _____(折扣)is a reduction in the usual price of something.

3. You can get a lot of _____(信息) from computers.

4. The deep snow made a lot of _____(不便)for drivers.

5. We learn a lot about Chinese _____(传统的)culture during we stay in Beijing.

6. If we have no computer, we will feel _____(convenient).

7. I find it much _____(easy) to translate English into Chinese.

8. Computer is one of the best _____(create)in modern civilization.

9. What job are you _____(interest) in?

10. He is as _____(tall)as me.

四、找出下列句子中错误的选项,并改正过来

1. We must study hard in order that serve the people better in the future.
　　　A　　　B　　　　　C　　D

2. It is more easier to make plans than to carry them out.
　　　A　　B　　　　　　　　C　　　　D

3. One of the students sit in front gave a different answer to the question.
　　　　　　A　　B　　　　C　　　　　　　　　D

4. My teacher told us to not talk loudly in the reading room.
　　　　　　A　　B　　　C　　　　D

5. The more he thought about it, the more questions he thought of ask.
　　　A　　　　B　　　　　　　　C　　　　　　D

6. It's kind for you to come to see us.
　　　A　　B　　C　　　D

7. Do you know who's English is the best in your class?
　　　　　　A　　　　B　　　C　　　D

Unit 3　Shopping

— 45 —

8. What time do Lily go to school every morning?
     A   B   C   D

9. The teacher told me that Mary did very good in drawing.
                A   B   C   D

10. David is one of those boys who is very helpful.
           A   B   C   D

单元检测

第一部分　英语知识运用(共分三节,满分 40 分)

第一节　语音知识:从 A、B、C、D 四个选项中找出其画线部分与所给单词画线部分读音相同的选项。(共 5 分,每小题 1 分)

(　　)1. h<u>o</u>nest　　A. h<u>i</u>story　　B. h<u>o</u>nor　　C. h<u>o</u>spital　　D. h<u>a</u>rm

(　　)2. <u>ex</u>cel　　A. <u>ex</u>perience　　B. <u>ex</u>ercise　　C. <u>ex</u>am　　D. <u>ex</u>cellent

(　　)3. ques<u>tion</u>　　A. na<u>tion</u>　　B. selec<u>tion</u>　　C. sugges<u>tion</u>　　D. sec<u>tion</u>

(　　)4. br<u>ea</u>k　　A. h<u>ea</u>t　　B. dis<u>ea</u>se　　C. gr<u>ea</u>t　　D. inst<u>ea</u>d

(　　)5. fl<u>oo</u>d　　A. c<u>oo</u>k　　B. bl<u>oo</u>d　　C. r<u>oo</u>m　　D. t<u>oo</u>th

第二节　词汇与语法知识:从 A、B、C、D 四个选项中选出可以填入空白处的最佳选项。(共 25 分,每小题 1 分)

(　　)6. Those old man are playing _____ basketball on the playground.

  A. a　　B. an　　C. the　　D. /

(　　)7. All the _____ in the college got presents yesterday.

  A. women teachers　　B. woman teachers

  C. women teacher　　D. woman teacher

(　　)8. This garden is _____ that one.

  A. ten times as long as　　B. ten times longer as

  C. ten times long as　　D. as longer ten times

(　　)9. —What can I do for you?

  —I want _____ orange blouse for my daughter.

  A. an　　B. the　　C. a　　D. /

(　　)10. Bob often _____ his mother with the housework on Sundays.

  A. help　　B. helping　　C. helps　　D. helped

(　　)11. —_____ you play golf?

—No, but I can play table tennis.

    A. Can   B. May   C. Must   D. Should

(   ) 12. This is _____ party that I have ever attended.

    A. the most wonderful   B. more wonderful

    C. wonderful   D. wonderfully

(   ) 13. She is one of _____ girls in her class.

    A. the youngest   B. the younger   C. the most young   D. young

(   ) 14. _____ interesting these books are!

    A. What   B. How   C. What an   D. How an

(   ) 15. I don't think _____ possible to master a foreign language without much memory work.

    A. it   B. its   C. that   D. this

(   ) 16. How can you keep the machine _____ when you are away.

    A. run   B. to run   C. running   D. being run

(   ) 17. No one can do it _____ he does.

    A. better than   B. better as   C good as   D. good than

(   ) 18. He wasn't _____ to lift the box.

    A. too strong   B. strong enough   C. enough strong   D. so strong

(   ) 19. _____ you do, _____ you get.

    A. The better; the more   B. The better; more

    C. Better; the more   D. Better; more

(   ) 20. Today he will leave _____ Beijing to visit his old friends.

    A. to   B. in   C. from   D. for

(   ) 21. —_____ will the manager come back to the company?

    —In two hours.

    A. How often   B. How long   C. How soon   D. How fast

(   ) 22. Tom speaks English _____ his uncle.

    A. as good as   B. as well as   C. as better as   D. as best as

(   ) 23. Hard working always _____ success.

    A. lead the way to   B. led the way of

    C. leads the way to   D. leads the way of

(   ) 24. The young teacher is popular _____ her students.

    A. for   B. at   C. with   D. from

(   )25. We can communicate _____ the people all over the world through the Internet.
   A. to   B. with   C. for   D. of

(   )26. How much do I need to _____ the three books?
   A. pay for   B. pay off   C. spend for   D. spend for

(   )27. He tried his best _____ the job well, he must be a good clerk.
   A. to do   B. doing   C. do   D. done

(   )28. He is one of the students that _____ passed the exam.
   A. has   B. have   C. is   D. are

(   )29. _____ the teacher's help, I got the first place this time.
   A. Thank to   B. Thanks for C. Thanks to   D. Thank for

(   )30. Both Tom and Mary _____ good at drawing pictures.
   A. is   B. are   C. was   D. being

第三节 完形填空: 阅读下面的短文,从所给的 A、B、C、D 四个选项中选出最佳的答案。(共10分,每小题1分)

Sam had a dog. Its name was Tod. It was very helpful, but it ate too much. So he didn't like it, he wanted to __31__ it. He __32__ Tod and put it in a small boat.

He rowed(划) the boat to the __33__ of a big river. Just as he __34__ the poor animal into the river, the boat began to go down. __35__ the man and Tod __36__ into the river.

Tod was able to swim, __37__ Sam couldn't. The dog bit the rope(绳子) and broke it. It tried its best to swim to __38__ Sam. The man was saved, so he was very thankful to the dog, he didn't want to kill the dog __39__. From then on, he gave the dog as __40__ as it wanted.

(   )31. A. sell   B. buy   C. beat   D. kill
(   )32. A. tied   B. pulled   C. pushed   D. closed
(   )33. A. front   B. foot   C. side   D. middle
(   )34. A. threw   B. carried   C. sent   D. brought
(   )35. A. Neither   B. Nor   C. Each   D. Both
(   )36. A. fell   B. swam   C. lost   D. jumped
(   )37. A. because   B. though   C. but   D. when
(   )38. A. kill   B. save   C. meet   D. hit
(   )39. A. no more   B. any more   C. no longer   D. not more
(   )40. A. little   B. few   C. many   D. much

第二部分 篇章与词汇理解(共分三节,满分50分)

第一节 阅读理解:阅读下列短文,从每题所给的A、B、C、D四个选项中选出最恰当的答案。(共30分,每小题2分)

A

Are you sure a cow can dance? Billy has one. It is an evening. Billy is giving a party at his home. All his friends are taking part in it. It is very hot. So many people are dancing outside in the garden. There is a house near the garden. The cows are sleeping there. But one cow can't sleep. She gets up and comes into the garden. She begins to dance. She dances very well. All the people stop dancing and watch her.

(   )41. Billy _____ in his home.
  A. is giving a lesson   B. is giving a party
  C. is dancing   D. is listening to the music

(   )42. All his friends _____.
  A. are taking part in the party   B. are dancing with him
  C. are giving a party   D. are singing

(   )43. Many people are dancing _____.
  A. out of the garden   B. in Billy's house
  C. near the garden   D. outside in the garden

(   )44. _____ are sleeping in the house near the garden.
  A. The cows   B. Bills'   C. All his friends   D. Many people

(   )45. One cow gets up and _____.
  A. listens to the music   B. begins to dance in the garden
  C. watch people dancing   D. come out of garden

B

I have many friends, and they have different favorite subjects. Jim's favorite subject is computer because he thinks computer can help him a lot in his study. He is a computer fan. He likes playing computer games very much, and he is good at playing them. Jack likes art best because he likes drawing pictures a lot. Mary likes Chinese because her mother is Chinese. Her mother teaches her Chinese at home. She loves China very much, and she wants to know more about China. Bob thinks math is very interesting, so he likes math very much. David likes P. E. Because he likes doing sports. He is good at playing basketball and <u>fencing</u>.

(   )46. How many friends are mentioned(被提到)in the passage?

A. Two.　　　　B. Three.　　　　C. Four.　　　　D. Five.

(　　)47. Jack likes art because he likes _____ a lot.
　　A. playing computer games　　　　B. taking photos
　　C. drawing pictures　　　　D. knowing more about China

(　　)48. What is Bob's favorite subject?
　　A. Computer.　　B. Chinese.　　C. Math.　　D. P. E.

(　　)49. What does the underlined word "fencing" mean?
　　A. 写作。　　B. 击剑。　　C. 插花。　　D. 烹煮。

(　　)50. The passage is mainly talking about _____.
　　A. the writer's friends and their favorite subjects
　　B. the writer's friends and their favorite food
　　C. the writer's parents and their favorite music
　　D. the writer's classmates and their favorite movies

C

In our city there is a big zoo. There are a lot of animals in it. There are some scary(吓人的) tigers and lions. They like eating meat and they eat much meat every day.

There are also two big elephants and a baby one. Children like to ride one of them. The elephants are very kind and friendly. They eat much grass and bananas.

In the zoo, we can see different kinds of bears, brown bears, black bears and white bears. They are all slow and stupid. They stand on their back legs and lift(抬高) their front legs to ask for food. They like cakes very much.

Do you like pandas? There's only one in the zoo. Her name is LingLing. She is very cute. She likes eating bamboo a lot. She is kind of shy. She's very interesting and lovely.

(　　)51. What do tigers and lions like eating?
　　A. Fruit.　　B. Meat.　　C. Vegetables.　　D. Rice.

(　　)52. How many elephants are there in the zoo?
　　A. One.　　B. Two.　　C. Three.　　D. Four.

(　　)53. What color are the bears in the zoo?
　　A. Black.　　B. Brown.　　C. White.　　D. A, B and C.

(　　)54. Bears stand on their _____ legs and lift their _____ legs to ask for food.
　　A. left; right　　B. right; left　　C. front; back　　D. back; front

(　　)55. Which one of the following is Not right?
　　A. Children like to ride on the elephants in the zoo.

B. The elephants are very friendly to people.

C. There is an elephant called LingLing.

D. Elephants like bananas very much.

第二节 词义搭配：从(B)栏中选出(A)栏单词的正确解释(共10分,每小题1分)

(A)　　　　　　　　　　　　(B)

(　　)56. add　　　　　　　A. exchange information each other

(　　)57. bestselling　　　　B. give sth. to sb. , supply

(　　)58. communication　　C. put two things together and find out difference

(　　)59. compare　　　　　D. sell well

(　　)60. offer　　　　　　　E. grade, degree

(　　)61. rating　　　　　　F. neither large nor small

(　　)62. tight　　　　　　　G. sth. about tradition

(　　)63. fit　　　　　　　　H. the thing used to do other things

(　　)64. traditional　　　　I. put one thing onto others

(　　)65. material　　　　　J. not relax

第三节 补全对话：根据对话内容,从对话后的选项中选出能填入空白处的最佳选项。(共10分,每小题2分)

Salesgirl: __66__ ?

Father: Yes, we'd like to have a look at mobile phone.

Salesgirl: OK, __67__ We have got NOKIA, SAMSUNG, PANDA, XIAXING and also other mobile phones from foreign countries.

Father : __68__ ?

Salesgirl: From 1,200 yuan to 3,000 yuan.

Father: What kind would you like to have, Zhang Lin?

Zhang Lin: I learned that SAMSUNG is very good.

Father: How much is it?

Salesgirl: __69__ . But I think you'd better buy a cheaper one. Because a type of new view-mobile will be instead of one at present. What about NOKIA? It's less than 1,500 yuan.

Father : __70__ ?

Salesgirl: Certainly. If there's anything wrong, you can turn it back.

Father : All right. We'll take it.

A. about 2,700 yuan
B. Is it good enough
C. How much are they
D. Here they are
E. Can I help you

第三部分 语言技能应用(共分四节,满分 30 分)

第一节 单词拼写:根据下列句子及所给汉语注释,在横线上写出该单词的正确形式。(共 5 分,每小题 1 分)

71. Please pay _____(注意) to your behavior.

72. He is willing to _____(接受) that fact that he didn't pass the test.

73. Good habits are good for the _____(发展) of teenagers.

74. The _____(政府) is discussing how to develop this area's economy.

75. Can e-books take the place of _____(传统的) books?

第二节 词形变换:用括号内单词的适当形式填空。(共 5 分,每小题 1 分)

76. The new shoes made his feet hurt, so he feel _____ (comfort).

77. _____ (luck), he missed the train again.

78. The _____ (friend) between our two countries will last forever.

79. Smoking is _____ (harm) to our health.

80. The war broke out in the early _____ (twenty) century.

第三节 改错:从 A、B、C、D 四个画线部分处找出一处错误的选项填入相应题号后的括号内,并在横线上写出正确答案。(共 10 分,每小题 2 分)

81. It is said that he used to spend five hours swim in the river.
        A   B   C   D

82. In fact, what they want to are just to make us pay more money.
   A   B   C   D

83. Could you tell me how can I get to the station?
    A   B C D

84. I think Tom went to the tower yesterday, do I?
    A   B   C   D

85. Father told me that light travelled faster than sound.
       A   B   C   D

第四节 书面表达。(共 10 分)

作文题目:Shopping on Line

词数要求:80~100 词

写作要点:1. 随着互联网的发展和普及,网络购物在中国也变得越来越普遍了,甚至已经成了我们日常生活中的一部分了;

2. 身边一定有不少同学已经通过网络进行购物了,比如淘宝网;

3. 网络购物的利与弊。

Unit 4

School Life

Warming up

一、句型汇总

1. What is your favorite subject at school? My favorite subject is…在学校里你最喜欢的学科是什么？我最喜欢的学科是……

2. Why do you like it so much? Because it is…为什么你如此喜欢它？因为它是……

3. What are you going to do after that? 在那以后你要做什么？

4. Shall we go together? 咱们一起去好吗？

5. Whether you want to get into a college or to become a skilled worker? 你是想上大学还是想成为一名技术工人？

6. You will study special subjects related to your major. 你也会学习一些与你的专业有关的学科。

　　relate 与……有关　relation 关系　relationship 关系　be related to 与……有关

7. You will learn and practice your skills in the training center.在技能培训中心你将会学习和练习你的技能。

　　practice v./n. 练习,实践　practice doing 练习做　put sth. into practice 把……投入实践

8. Life at school is not all about studying. 学校生活不是都与学习有关。not all 不是所有的

9. Having fun can help you relax and help you learn. 娱乐能帮助你放松也能帮助你学习。help sb. do sth./help sb. to do sth. 帮助某人做某事。

10. Vocational high school students need to pay special attention to practical training, because learning skills in the training center is as important as learning things in the classroom. 职业学校的学生需要特别注意技能练习,因为在训练中心学习技能和在教室学习是一样重要的。

  pay attention to 注意…… as important as 和……一样重要

11. Many school activities are not related to study, students should not spend their time on them. 许多学校活动与学习无关,学生不应该把时间花费在这些事上.

  spend…on 在……上花费

12. So, it sounds like vocational high schools are not so different from normal high schools. 所以,听起来职业中学与普通中学是不同的。

  be different from… 和……不同

13. About half of its students choose to have vocational education after leaving secondary school. 在初中毕业以后大约一半的学生都选择职业教育。

  choose to do 选择去做

14. Students apply to a real company which offers training in that occupation. 学生向那些能够提供相关职业培训的真实公司做出申请。

  apply to 向……申请   apply for 申请   application   n. 申请

二、英汉互译

1. information technology _____   2. enjoy doing _____
3. a lot of fun _____   4. useful and interesting _____
5. have class _____   6. hold a competition _____
7. from…to… _____   8. 上技能训练课 _____
9. 基础学科 _____   10. 为……做准备 _____
11. 从……中选择 _____   12. 与……有关 _____

Listening and Speaking

一、找出与所给单词画线部分读音相同的选项

(　　) 1. che<u>m</u>istry   A. <u>ch</u>ange   B. tea<u>ch</u>   C. <u>ch</u>icken   D. te<u>ch</u>nology

(　　) 2. f<u>u</u>n   A. h<u>u</u>ge   B. comp<u>u</u>ter   C. p<u>o</u>pular   D. p<u>u</u>blic

(　　) 3. relat<u>ed</u>   A. decid<u>ed</u>   B. turn<u>ed</u>   C. pick<u>ed</u>   D. practic<u>ed</u>

(　　) 4. grow<u>th</u>   A. too<u>th</u>   B. <u>th</u>ough   C. al<u>th</u>ough   D. <u>th</u>us

( )5. major   A. hall   B. practice   C. related   D. hands-on

二、从 B 栏中找出与 A 栏中相对应的答语

A

1. What is your favorite subject at a school?
2. Why do you like it so much?
3. What are you going to do tomorrow?
4. Shall we go together?
5. Do you spend all your time at school learning and training?

B

A. Of course not.
B. Sure. It'll be great.
C. My favorite subject is P. E.
D. Because it is very funny.
E. I'm going to watch the movie with my friends.

三、用所给句子补全下面对话

A：Good morning, sir! Can I help you?

B：Good morning! I want to spend my vacation abroad.

A：__1__

B：I have no idea. I'm too tired and just want to relax.

A：__2__

B：Russia is too cold now. Any other good places?

A：What about Australia?

B：__3__

A：There is a lot of sunshine there all the year round.

B：OK. __4__

A：How long will you spend your vacation?

B：For one month.

A：__5__

B：All right.

A. What about Russia?
B. Which country do you like to visit?
C. What's the weather like there?
D. I'll call you as soon as I get the plan for you.
E. Make a travel plan to Australia for me.

四、场景模拟

编写一组对话,和朋友谈论一下你的学校生活。

提示词汇:my favorite subject is...
I like it because... enjoy...class very much
a lot of fun   useful and interesting
the development plan for a new product
work report   prepare for the meeting

_____
_____
_____
_____
_____
_____

Reading and Writing

一、用括号内所给汉语提示或单词的适当形式填空

1. Besides Chinese, we learn some other subjects, _____（化学）for example.

2. Next week, we will have a singing _____（比赛）.

3. The _____（实习）in this company is very interesting and useful.

4. I come to this school to learn special _____（技能）.

5. My _____（最喜爱的）food is dumplings.

6. The students are practicing _____（sing）English songs.

7. If you feel too tired, you can listen to some _____（relax）music.

8. In order to make rapid progress, we did a lot of _____（relate）practical training.

9. When they hear the good news, all the boys are _____（excite）.

10. My uncle has become an _____（experience）chemist.

二、完形填空

Being lame(瘸的), I didn't dare to walk in front of my classmates. I was afraid that I might be　1　at. In those days I was very sad to see others walking　2　.

One day, a few students came up to me and asked me to go outside. I was really　3　. They encouraged me with a(n)　4　smile and　5　me in my wheelchair from place to place. I was　6　to them for giving me a chance to see the　7　of our lovely school with my own eyes.

After that we ofen read, played and talked together. My friends are always　8　to help me It made me　9　I am disabled(残疾的).

Once they asked me, "What is the most beautiful thing in our school?" Without hesitation(犹豫) I said, "It is the　10　."

(　　)1. A. laughed　　B. smiled　　C. stared　　D. looked
(　　)2. A. quickly　　B. slowly　　C. happily　　D. shyly
(　　)3. A. brave　　B. sad　　C. hurt　　D. excited
(　　)4. A. honest　　B. friendly　　C. luckily　　D. handsome
(　　)5. A. pushed　　B. placed　　C. drew　　D. pulled
(　　)6. A. satisfied　　B. sorry　　C. pleased　　D. grateful
(　　)7. A. signs　　B. sights　　C. buildings　　D. students
(　　)8. A. ready　　B. smart　　C. wise　　D. unwilling
(　　)9. A. forget　　B. remember　　C. imagine　　D. think
(　　)10. A. teachers　　B. schoolyard　　C. classmates　　D. friendship

三、阅读理解

阅读下面短文,从每题所给的 A、B、C、D 四个选项中选出最佳答案。

Last Tuesday, after doing some shopping in town, I wanted to have a rest before going back home. So I bought a newspaper and some chocolate and went into a coffee shop to sit at a long table. I put my heavy bag down on the floor, put the newspaper and chocolate on the table, and went to get a cup of coffee.

When I came back with my coffee, there wasa young man sitting next to me. It was one of those strange-looking young men, with dark glasses, torn clothes, and long hair. But I wasn't surprised at such a young man. What surprised me most was that he had started to eat my chocolate!

I was rather uneasy about him, but I didn't want to get into trouble. I just looked down at the front page of the newspaper and took a bit of chocolate. The young man looked at me. Then he took a second piece of my chocolate. I could hardly believe it. Still I didn't say anything. When he took a third one, I felt more angry than uneasy. I thought, "Well, I shall have the last piece." And I got it.

The young man gave me a strange look and then stood up. As he left, he shouted out, "This woman is crazy!" Everyone looked at me. That was embarrassing enough. But it was worse when I finished my coffee and ready to leave. It wasn't my chocolate that I had eaten a moment before. Mine was just under my newspaper.

(　　) 1. The woman went to town to _____.

   A. catch the train   B. buy some chocolate and coffee

   C. have a rest   D. do some shopping

(　　) 2. The woman was unhappy because _____.

   A. the train was late

   B. she was afraid of the young man

   C. she thought the young man was eating her chocolate

   D. she couldn't find her coffee

(　　) 3. What does the word uneasy mean?

   A. 不容易。 B. 不自在。 C. 不舒服。 D. 不自然。

(　　) 4. According to the story, who got angry at last?

   A. The young man.   B. The woman.

   C. Neither of them.   D. Both of them.

(　　) 5. The woman found she had made a mistake _____.

   A. just after she saw the young man next to her

   B. when the young man was leaving

   C. after she finished reading her newspaper

   D. right before she was about to leave the coffee shop

四、书面表达。

作文题目:Surfing the Internet

词数要求:80~100 词

写作要点:1. 随着网络的普及,青少年越来越喜欢上网;

    2. 你对上网有哪些看法。

Grammar

一、从下面每小题四个选项中选出最佳选项

(   ) 1. There _____ a meeting tomorrow afternoon.
   A. will be going to   B. will going to be
   C. is going to be   D. will go to be

(   ) 2. Charlie _____ here next month.
   A. isn't working   B. doesn't working
   C. isn't going to working D. won't work

(   ) 3. He _____ very busy this week, he _____ free next week.
   A. will be; is   B. is; is
   C. will be; will be   D. is; will be

(   ) 4. There _____ a dolphin show in the zoo tomorrow evening.
   A. was   B. is going to have
   C. will have   D. is going to be

(   ) 5. —_____ you _____ free tomorrow?
   —No. I _____ free the day after tomorrow.
   A. Are; going to; will   B. Are; going to be; will
   C. Are; going to; will be D. Are; going to be; will be

(   ) 6. Mother _____ me a nice present on my next birthday.
   A. will gives   B. will give   C. gives   D. give

(   ) 7. —Shall I buy a cup of tea for you?
   —_____. (不, 不要。)
   A. No, you won't   B. No, you aren't
   C. No, please don't   D. No, please

(   ) 8. —Where is the morning paper?
   —I _____ it for you at once.
   A. get   B. am getting   C. to get   D. will get

(   ) 9. _____ a concert next Saturday?
   A. There will be   B. Will there be   C. There can be   D. There are

(   ) 10. If they come, we _____ a meeting.

A. have   B. will have   C. had   D. would have

( ) 11. He _____ her a beautiful hat on her next birthday.
   A. gives   B. gave   C. will giving   D. is going to give

( ) 12. He _____ to us as soon as he gets there.
   A. writes   B. has written   C. will write   D. wrote

( ) 13. He _____ in three days.
   A. coming back   B. came back
   C. will come back   D. is going to coming back

( ) 14. If it _____ tomorrow, we'll go roller-skating.
   A. isn't rain   B. won't rain   C. doesn't rain   D. doesn't fine

( ) 15. —Will his parents go to see the Terra Cotta Warriors tomorrow?
   —No, _____ (不去).
   A. they willn't.   B. they won't.   C. they aren't   D. they don't.

( ) 16. Who _____ we _____ swimming with tomorrow afternoon?
   A. will; go to   B. do; go   C. will; going   D. shall; go

( ) 17. We _____ the work this way next time.
   A. do   B. will do   C. going to do   D. will doing

( ) 18. Tomorrow he _____ a kite in the open air first, and then _____ boating in the park.
   A. will fly; will go   B. will fly; goes
   C. is going to fly; will goes   D. flies; will go

( ) 19. The day after tomorrow they _____ a volleyball match.
   A. will watching   B. watches   C. will watch   D. watch

( ) 20. There _____ a birthday party this Sunday.
   A. shall be   B. will be
   C. shall going to be   D. will going to be

( ) 21. They _____ an English evening next Sunday.
   A. are having   B. are going to have
   C. will having   D. is going to have

( ) 22. _____ you _____ free next Sunday?
   A. Will; are   B. Will; be   C. Do; be   D. Are; be

( ) 23. He _____ there at ten tomorrow morning.
   A. will   B. is   C. will be   D. be

( ) 24. _____ your brother _____ a magazine from the library?

A. Are；going to borrow　　　　B. Is；going to borrow
C. Will；borrows　　　　　　　　D. Are；going to borrows

(　　)25. —Shall I come again tomorrow afternoon?
　　　　 —_____（好的）.
　　　　 A. Yes, please　　B. Yes, you will　　C. No, please　　D. No, you won't

(　　)26. It _____ the year of the horse next year.
　　　　 A. is going to be　　B. is going to　　C. will be　　D. will is

(　　)27. _____ open the window?
　　　　 A. Will you please　　B. Please will you　　C. You please　　D. Do you

(　　)28. —Let's go out to play football, shall we?
　　　　 —OK. I _____.
　　　　 A. will coming　　　　　　B. be going to come
　　　　 C. come　　　　　　　　　D. am coming

(　　)29. It _____ us a long time to learn English well.
　　　　 A. takes　　B. will take　　C. spends　　D. will spend

(　　)30. The train _____ at 11.
　　　　 A. going to arrive　　B. will be arrive　　C. is going to　　D. is arriving

二、找出下列句子中错误的选项,并改正过来

1. It won't be long before they will get married.
　 A　　 B　　　　　 C　　　　 D

2. Are you join us if we decide to do the new experiment?
　 A　　 B　　　　　 C　　　　　　　　 D

3. It'll be some time when the buildings is completed.
　　　　 A　　　 B　　 C　　　　　　　 D

4. I leave in a minute. I must finish all my work before I leave.
　 A　　　　　　　　　　 B　　　　　　　 C　　　 D

5. —How long do you study in our country? —I plan to be here for about one more year.
　　　　　 A　　　 B　　　　　　　　　　　 C　 D

6. —What are you do after you leave here? —I will return home to work.
　　　　 A　　 B　　　　　　　　　　　　　 C　　　　　　 D

7. I am tired. I am go to bed early tonight.
　 A　　　　　 B C　　　　　　 D

8. Mary's birthday is next Monday, her mother is giving her a present.
　 A　　　　　　 B　　　　　　　　　　 C　　　　　　 D

9. It is very cold these days. It is snowing soon.
　 A B　　　　　 C　　　　 D

10. —Have you be here this Saturday? —No. I will visit my teacher.
　　　　 A　　 B　　　 C　　　　　　　　　 D

For Better Performance

一、找出与所给单词画线部分读音相同的选项

(　　)1. r<u>u</u>de　　A. f<u>u</u>n　　B. s<u>u</u>bject　　C. bl<u>u</u>e　　D. th<u>u</u>mb

(　　)2. inform<u>a</u>tion　　A. m<u>a</u>jor　　B. pr<u>a</u>ctice　　C. rel<u>a</u>xing　　D. h<u>a</u>ll

(　　)3. <u>e</u>xperience　　A. <u>e</u>xciting　　B. <u>e</u>xample　　C. <u>e</u>xercise　　D. <u>e</u>xpert

(　　)4. maj<u>or</u>　　A. invent<u>or</u>　　B. sh<u>or</u>t　　C. rep<u>or</u>t　　D. imp<u>or</u>tant

(　　)5. phy<u>s</u>ics　　A. politic<u>s</u>　　B. practi<u>c</u>e　　C. redu<u>c</u>e　　D. <u>s</u>cience

二、英汉互译

1. an internship at a company _____
2. go on a school trip _____
3. join a school club _____
4. finish a work report _____
5. make a preparation for the discussion _____
6. 在技能培训中心练习技能_____
7. 最重要的事情_____
8. 与……不同_____
9. 学习技术的好方法_____
10. 当然_____
11. 决定去做_____
12. 不多于_____

三、用括号内所给汉语提示或单词的适当形式填空

1. My dream is to go to an excellent _____(大学).
2. Our team won the football game. It's really an _____(令人兴奋的)news.
3. _____(练习)makes perfect. It is a truth forever.
4. My father is a teacher. He teaches _____(政治)in a normal high school.
5. Don't disturb him. He is _____(准备)for the coming exam.
6. Before you make a _____(决定),you must think it over.
7. Little Tom is _____(interesting)in the science experiment.
8. After doing a lot of practice,he is a _____(skill)worker now.
9. Mrs Brown is experienced in _____(make)fashionable clothes.
10. His way of solving this problem sounds like _____(use).

四、找出下列句子中错误的选项,并改正过来

1. This accident must be related with Tom's careless driving.
                A   B   C   D

2. Spoken English is different in written English in many ways.
      A   B   C   D

3. Physics are not so difficult to learn.
      A   B   C   D

4. Zhang Yuchen enjoys to play basketball, but John likes playing chess.
             A   B   C   D

5. He was too tired to not walk any further.
      A   B   C   D

单元检测

第一部分 英语知识运用(共分三节,满分40分)

第一节 语音知识:从 A、B、C、D 四个选项中找出其画线部分与所给单词画线部分读音相同的选项。(共5分,每小题1分)

( ) 1. hour   A. honest   B. healthy   C. happiness   D. unhappy

( ) 2. appear   A. bear   B. disappear   C. pear   D. wear

( ) 3. exam   A. exciting   B. experience   C. excellent   D. example

( ) 4. fun   A. student   B. supply   C. but   D. useful

( ) 5. politics   A. compare   B. communicate   C. shop   D. mother

第二节 词汇与语法知识:从 A、B、C、D 四个选项中选出可以填入空白处的最佳选项。(共25分,每小题1分)

( ) 6. _____ girl riding a bike is _____ college student.
    A. The; a   B. A; the   C. A; an   D. The; an

( ) 7. A young man is practicing _____ English with Kathy in the garden.
    A. to speak   B. saying   C. speaking   D. to say

( ) 8. I enjoy _____ books.
    A. looking   B. to look   C. reading   D. to read

( ) 9. Everyone will _____ mistakes in his life.
    A. make   B. take   C. get   D. have

( ) 10. I look forward to _____ from you soon.

A. hear　　　B. hearing　　　C. hears　　　D. heard

( ) 11. He _____ his mistake until his friend told him.

A. didn't pay attention to　　　B. wasn't pay attention to

C. didn't pay attention that　　　D. wasn't pay attention that

( ) 12. He decides _____ to Hong Kong on vacation.

A. to go　　　B. going　　　C. gone　　　D. go

( ) 13. _____ you want to get into a college or to become a skilled worker?

A. Whether　　　B. If　　　C. What　　　D. Who

( ) 14. —Why she made her parents so angry?

—_____ she had failed in the examination.

A. As　　　B. Because　　　C. Since　　　D. That

( ) 15. This film is _____ that one.

A. as interesting as　　　B. as more interesting as

C. as interested as　　　D. as more interested as

( ) 16. When he is twenty, he _____ a famous dancer.

A. is becoming　　　B. will become　　　C. to become　　　D. should become

( ) 17. The document _____ the workers' salary is very reasonable.

A. related　　　B. related to　　　C. relating on　　　D. related with

( ) 18. _____, they add 200 dollars to the workers.

A. In add　　　B. On addition　　　C. In addition　　　D. On add

( ) 19. Look at the black cloud, it _____ rain.

A. is going to　　　B. will be　　　C. shall be　　　D. are going to

( ) 20. I will tell you the truth if he _____.

A. leave　　　B. will leave　　　C. leaves　　　D. left

( ) 21. There will be an English speech contest, _____?

A. isn't it　　　B. aren't there　　　C. won't there　　　D. didn't there

( ) 22. I plan _____ to Beijing for the Summer vacation.

A. go　　　B. to go　　　C. going　　　D. gone

( ) 23. I can't help _____ the heavy box, because my leg is broken.

A. carry　　　B. to carry　　　C. carrying　　　D. caught

( ) 24. Life at school is not all about studying. _____ can help you relax and help you learn.

A. Having fun　　　B. Have fun　　　C. To have fun　　　D. Have funny

( )25. You will study basic subjects _____ Politics, Chinese, Math, English and History.
  A. for example B. such as C. such like D. just as

( )26. I often see the old man _____ his dog in the park.
  A. running B. run C. walking D. walk

( )27. You will also get hand-on experience by _____ internships at real companies.
  A. do B. to do C. doing D. done

( )28. Students _____ a real company which offers training in that occupation.
  A. want to B. go to C. apply to D. are going to

( )29. It is necessary _____ students _____ two languages.
  A. of; mastering B. of; to master C. for; mastering D. for; to master

( )30. She sees _____ high buildings _____ she can't believe her eyes.
  A. so; that B. so; that C. such; that D. such; that

第三节　完形填空：阅读下面的短文，从所给的 **A、B、C、D** 四个选项中选出正确的答案。(共10分,每题1分)

Have you ever seen a rainbow in the sky? Do you know what it is?

A story says that when you see a rainbow you should __31__ at once to the place where it touches the ground, and __32__ you would find a bag of gold. Of course, it is not __33__. You could not find the bag of gold, nor could you ever find its end. No matter how __34__ you run, it always seems far away.

A rainbow is not a thing which we can feel with our __35__ as we can feel a flower. It is only the effect of light shining on raindrops. The raindrops catch the sunlight and break it up into all the wonderful colors which we see.

It is __36__ a rainbow perhaps because it is made up of raindrops and looks like a bow. That is __37__ we can never see a rainbow in a clear __38__. We see rainbows __39__ when there is rain in the air and the sun is shining brightly through the clouds. Every rainbow has many colors in the same order. The first of the top color is always red, next __40__ orange, then green, and last of all blue. A rainbow is indeed one of the wonders of nature.

( )31. A. run B. walk C. jump D. stand
( )32. A. where B. there C. here D. near
( )33. A. good B. wrong C. beautiful D. true
( )34. A. long B. short C. far D. difficult
( )35. A. hands B. legs C. heads D. eyes

( )36. A. called   B. spoken   C. meant   D. asked
( )37. A. because   B. why   C. so   D. that
( )38. A. space   B. sky   C. fields   D. water
( )39. A. hardly   B. really   C. only   D. usually
( )40. A. goes   B. sees   C. covers   D. comes

第二部分　篇章与词汇理解(共分三节,满分50分)

第一节　阅读理解:阅读下面的短文,从每题所给的A、B、C、D四个选项中选出最恰当的答案。(共30分,每小题2分)

A

Mr. Hodges was the owner and editor(编辑) of a small newspaper. He always tried to bring his readers the latest news.

One day, he received an exciting telephone call from someone who claimed that he had great detail, and Mr. Hodges wrote it all down and printed it in his paper that evening. He was delighted to see that no other paper had got hold of the story.

Unfortunately, however, angry telephone calls soon showed that he had been tricked, so in the next day's paper he wrote: "We were the first and only newspaper to report yesterday that the village of Green bridge had been destroyed by a flood. Today, we are proud to say that we are again the first newspaper to bring our readers the news that yesterday's story was quite false."

( )41. What did Mr. Hodges always try to bring to his readers?
　　　A. A small newspaper　　　　B. Detective stories
　　　C. A lot of pleasure　　　　D. The latest news

( )42. What was the news that someone gave Mr. Hodges one day?
　　　A. A serious drought near Green bridge.
　　　B. A lot of people were killed and the ground was covered with flood.
　　　C. A big flood up in the mountain.
　　　D. Yesterday's story was quite false.

( )43. How did some readers feel when they read the news printed in Hodges' newspapers?
　　　A. Surprised.　　B. Angry.　　C. Delighted.　　D. Happy.

( )44. What did Mr. Hodges find later?
　　　A. He had been deceived.
　　　B. He should have set out to investigate the incident.

C. He wished that he had tried every way to get the news confirmed.

D. He was right in printing the news he received from the call.

(　　)45. What do you think of Mr. Hodges?

　　　A. He's a fortunate person.　　　B. He's a poor editor.

　　　C. He's a very good writer.　　　D. He's not easy to be deceived.

B

Do you know something about tree rings? Do you know they can tell us what the weather was like, sometimes even hundreds of years ago? A tree will grow well in a climate with lots of sunshine and rainfall. And little sunshine or rainfall will limit the growth of a tree. We can see the change of climate(气候) by studying the tree rings. For example, to find out the weather of ten years ago, count the rings of a tree from the outside to the most of that year. If it is near to the eleventh ring, then the climate that year was bad.

Tree rings are important not only for studying the history of weather but also for studying the history of man. Many centuries ago there lived a lot of people at a place in New Mexico. But now you can find only sand there — no trees and no people. What happened? A scientist studied the rings of dead trees there. He found that the people had to leave because they had cut down all the trees to make fires and buildings. As all the trees had gone, the people there had to move.

(　　)46. _____ in good climate.

　　　A. Tree rings grow far from each other

　　　B. Tree rings become thinner

　　　C. Trees don't need sunshine or rainfall

　　　D. People can cut down most of the trees

(　　)47. The scientists are interested in studying tree rings because tree rings can tell _____.

　　　A. whether a tree was strong or not

　　　B. whether people took good care of the trees or not

　　　C. whether the climate was good or not

　　　D. how old the trees were

(　　)48. If you want to find out the weather of twenty years ago, you should study _____.

　　　A. the twentieth ring　　　B. the tenth ring

　　　C. the nineteenth ring　　　D. the twenty-first ring

(　　)49. Why did people usually live in places with lots of trees?

　　　A. Trees could tell the change of the weather.

　　　B. Trees brought lots of sunshine and rain.

C. Trees could make weather not too hot or too cold.

D. Trees could be used for burning and for building house.

(   )50. The people had to leave the place in New Mexico because _____.

A. bad weather stopped the growth of trees

B. they no longer had water and the land became sand

C. they didn't have enough trees for burning

D. there was too much rain there

C

It was the last day of the final examination in a college. On the steps of building, a group of engineering students were waiting for the last exam. On their faces was confidence. They knew the exam would be easy. The professor had said they could bring any books or notes during the test.

Right after they came into the classroom, the professor handed out the papers. There were only five questions on it.

Three hours passed. Then the professor began to collect the papers. the students no longer looked confident. On their faces was nervous expression. The professor watched the worried faces before him, and then asked, "How many of you have completed all five questions?" No hand was raised. "How many of you have answered four?" Still no hands. "Three? Two?" The students moved restlessly in their seats. "One, then? Certainly somebody has finished one." But the class kept silent. The professor said, " That is exactly what I just want to make you know clearly that even though you have completed four years of engineering. There are still many things about the subject you don't know. These questions you could not answer are common in everyday practice." Then, smiling, he added, " you will all pass this course, your education has just begun. "

The years have <u>obscured</u> the name of this professor, but not the lesson he taught.

(   )51. Why did the students think the exam was easy at first?

A. Because it was their last exam in the college.

B. Because they knew there were only five questions.

C. Because they thought they were clever and talented.

D. Because they were allowed to bring any books and notes during the test.

(   )52. How many students have finished all the five questions?

A. All of them.　　B. Some of them.　　C. None of them.　　D. Only one of them.

(   )53. What does the underline word"obscured" mean in the last paragraph?

A. 模糊。　　　B. 回忆。　　　C. 提醒。　　　D. 改变。

(   )54. What could the students learn from the last exam?

A. He laughs best who laughs last.

B. A good beginning is half done.

C. One is never too old to learn.

D. The early bird catches the worm.

( )55. What's the best title for the article?

A. Some Confident Students.　　B. An Engineering Exam.

C. An Interesting Professor.　　D. An Unforgettable Lesson.

第二节　词义搭配:从(B)栏中选出(A)栏单词的正确解释。(共10分,每小题1分)

(A)　　　　　　　　　　　(B)

(　)56. college　　　　　　A. seem, as if

(　)57. interesting　　　　B. something with a lot of interest

(　)58. internship　　　　 C. a subject about computer and internet

(　)59. relaxing　　　　　 D. like best

(　)60. special　　　　　　E. unlike others

(　)61. Information technology　F. practice, training

(　)62. favorite　　　　　 G. not tight

(　)63. competition　　　　H. do sth. for the thing happened future

(　)64. prepare　　　　　　I. contest, compete with others

(　)65. sound like　　　　 J. a place for higher education, university

第三节　补全对话:根据对话内容,从对话后的选项中选出能填入空白处的最佳选项。(共10分,每小题2分)

A. Hello, Maria! Long time no see!

B. I'm busy these days.

A. What a beautiful new skirt you wear today!

B. Thank you.　66　

A. Of course. Where did you buy it?

B.　67

A. You didn't buy it? Is it a gift from your parents?

B. No.　68

A. Really? I can't believe it!

B.　69　I enjoy making clothes by myself. My mother is really good at making clothes and she taught me a lot about it.　70　the color and design were very nice to me. I made a skirt with it by myself.

A. Wow, what a clever girl you are!

— 70 —

A. I didn't buy it.

B. Last Sunday I bought a piece of cloth(布).

C. I'm not kidding.

D. I made it by myself.

E. I like it too.

F. Do you really think so?

第三部分　语言技能运用(共分4节,满分30分)

第一节　单词拼写:根据下列句子及所给中文注释,在横线上写出该单词的正确形式。(共5分,每小题1分)

71. Since English is a tool for communication, we should pay more _____ (注意力) to spoken English.

72. You can get a lot of _____ (信息) from the internet.

73. Some people think that smoking makes them feel happy and helps them _____ (放松).

74. The pretty girl told me about her _____ (最喜爱的) subject.

75. We should remember the China-Japan War's _____ (历史).

第二节　词形变换:用括号内所给词的适当形式填空。(共5分,每小题1分)

76. A good _____ (begin) is half done.

77. What job are you _____ (interest) in?

78. Mr Black is an _____ (experience) English teacher.

79. Do you know who is _____ (relate) to the case.

80. One person can make a _____ (different) by saving energy.

第三节　改错:从 A、B、C、D 四个画线部分处找出一处错误的选项填入相应题号后的括号内,并在横线上写出正确答案。(共10分,每小题2分)

81. He is leaving Beijing for Paris tomorrow.
　　　A　　B　　　　C　　　D

82. There will not have enough rooms for such a large population in the future.
　　　　　　A　　　　B　　　　C　　　　D

83. "You are late for school unless you get up at five." said mother.
　　　　A　　B　　　C　　　D

84. This is one of the most exciting football games which I have ever seen.
　　　A　　　B　　　　　　　　　C　　D

85. In the evening of Christmas, the little girl lost her life because of cold weather.
　　A　　　　　　　　　　　　　B　C　　　　D

第四节　书面表达。(共10分)

作文题目:My School Life

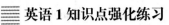

词数要求:80~100 词

写作要点:1. 描述你的学校生活;

2. 谈谈你的感受。

Unit 5

Celebrations

Warming up

一、句型汇总

1. This is Zixuan. 这是梓轩。

2. How are you? 你好吗？

3. How about you? 你呢？

4. What can I do for you? 我能为你做什么呢？

5. I want to invite you to a welcome banquet tomorrow evening. 我想邀请你参加明晚的欢迎宴会。

6. Do you have time? 你有时间吗？

二、英汉互译

1. banquet _____   2. 生日晚会_____

3. invite _____   4. 开幕式_____

5. welcome banquet _____   6. 欢迎晚会_____

7. how about _____   8. 希望_____

9. of course _____   10. 好极了_____

Listening and Speaking

一、找出与所给单词画线部分读音相同的选项

(　　) 1. c<u>a</u>feteria　　A. pr<u>a</u>ctice　　B. f<u>a</u>vorite　　C. <u>a</u>ssistant　　D. m<u>a</u>terial

(　　) 2. c<u>o</u>mmon　　A. c<u>o</u>nfirm　　B. s<u>o</u>und　　C. p<u>o</u>litics　　D. c<u>o</u>mpete

(　　) 3. b<u>a</u>nquet　　A. <u>a</u>ddress　　B. sp<u>e</u>cial　　C. <u>c</u>hemistry　　D. <u>e</u>xperience

(　　) 4. invit<u>a</u>tion　　A. sn<u>a</u>ck　　B. c<u>e</u>lebrate　　C. tr<u>a</u>ditional　　D. pr<u>a</u>ctical

(　　) 5. b<u>ea</u>t　　A. f<u>ea</u>ture　　B. sw<u>ea</u>ter　　C. d<u>ea</u>d　　D. br<u>ea</u>th

二、从 B 栏中找出与 A 栏中相对应的答语

A	B
1. How are you?	A. Yes, I'd love to.
2. Do you have time this Saturday?	B. I'm great. Thanks.
3. When and where will the party be held?	C. Of course. I know a perfect game for welcome parties.
4. Would you like to come to our party?	D. Yes, I have time. I'll be there.
5. Can you give us some ideas for the party activities?	E. At 10 o'clock in the cafeteria.

三、用所给句子补全下面对话

A：Hi, Li Xia. It is very kind of you to invite me to your home.

B：Make yourself at home please.

A：All your family are busy cleaning the house. ___1___

B：Yes, please. You can help me put up these paper-cuts.

A：OK. ___2___

B：We want to sweep away bad things. Then we will have good luck in the new year.

A：It sounds great. Does the Spring Festival mean a lot to Chinese people?

B：Of course. ___3___ To prepare for the festival, we will clean the house and buy presents!

A：___4___

B：On Spring Festival Eve, we often get together to have a big dinner.

A：What else?

B：People will give best wishes to each other by saying things such as "Happy New Year".

A：___5___

B：Happy New Year!

> A. Why do you clean the house before the Spring Festival?
> B. Oh, now I should say Happy New Year!
> C. Do you need any help?
> D. The Spring Festival is the most important festival in China.
> E. I wonder what Chinese people do to celebrate the festival?

四、场景模拟

编写一组对话，端午节假期前，李明向外籍同学 Peter 介绍中国端午节，并邀请 Peter 到家中一起庆祝该节日。

提示词汇：Dragon Boat Festival, a history of more than 2,000 years, in memory of Qu Yuan, eat zongzi, watch dragon boat racing.

Reading and Writing

一、用括号内所给汉语提示或单词的适当形式填空

1. Your _____（支持）has played an important role in our company's growth.

2. I would like to invite you to attend the _____（open）ceremony of our new shopping mall in Shenzhen.

3. The event will be _____（hold）at 108 Nanping Road.

4. I _____（真诚地）hope you will come with us.

5. We have been business _____（partner）for over ten years.

6. We want to take this _____（机会）to thank you.

7. I look forward to _____ (see) you tomorrow.

8. On _____ (代表) of my colleagues and myself, I thank you.

9. We hope you will be able to _____ (确认) your attendance before October 8th.

10. I appreciate your _____ (invite).

二、完形填空

Songkran Festival is a very important festival in Thailand. Thai people __1__ it Tai New Year, too. It is from April 13th to April 15th every year. __2__ that time, Thai people usually go back home to __3__ the festival with their family. The word Songkran __4__ "to move" or "to change". It is the day __5__ the sun changes its position in the zodiac(黄道带). Thai people also call Songkran Festival "Water Festival", because they always celebrate the festival with __6__. They throw water at each __7__. And they think water can __8__ away bad luck of the old year and bring good luck to the new year. Songkran Festival is __9__ a time for Thai people to clean their houses. If you go to Thailand during Songkran Festival, you can see many Thai people sing and __10__ on the street.

( ) 1. A. call   B. calls   C. called   D. calling
( ) 2. A. In   B. On   C. At   D. Of
( ) 3. A. celebrate   B. celebrates   C. celebrating   D. celebrated
( ) 4. A. meaning   B. meaningful   C. meaningless   D. means
( ) 5. A. which   B. when   C. that   D. where
( ) 6. A. water   B. beer   C. juice   D. wine
( ) 7. A. another   B. others   C. the other   D. other
( ) 8. A. blow   B. throw   C. wash   D. take
( ) 9. A. also   B. too   C. either   D. neither
( ) 10. A. dances   B. dance   C. danced   D. dancing

三、阅读理解

Chinese Dragon Boat Festival is also known as Duanwu Festival. It's one of the three most important lunar festivals in China, along with Spring Festival and Mid-Autumn Festival.

The date of the festival is said to be the date when Qu Yuan died—the fifth day of the fifth lunar month, so the date varies from year to year, such as it is June 20 in 2015, June 9 in 2016, May 30 in 2017, June 18 in 2018, June 7 in 2019, June 25 in 2020 and June 14 in 2021.

Although the date is different, the custom is the same. With a history of over 2,000 years, people celebrate it with all kinds of activities on that day. They hold dragon boat racing, eat zongzi, drink realgar wine (雄黄酒), wear sachets (香囊) and so on. But dragon boat racing is the most popular activity during the Dragon Boat Festival.

(　　)1. Which of the following is NOT the most important lunar festival in China?
　　A. May Day.　　　　　　　　　B. Dragon Boat Festival.
　　C. Spring Festival.　　　　　　D. Mid-Autumn Festival.

(　　)2. The underlined word "varies" in the passage means"_____" in Chinese.
　　A. 相似。　　B. 变化。　　C. 推迟。　　D. 递进。

(　　)3. Dragon Boat Festival is on _____ in 2021.
　　A. June 20　　B. May 30　　C. June 7　　D. June 14

(　　)4. How long has Chinese people celebrated the Dragon Boat Festival?
　　A. For about 2,000 years.　　　　B. For almost 2,500 years.
　　C. For less than 2,000 years.　　D. For more than 2,000 years.

(　　)5. _____ is the most popular activity during the Dragon Boat Festival.
　　A. Drinking realgar wine　　　　B. Eating zongzi
　　C. Dragon boat racing　　　　　D. Wearing sachets

四、书面表达

假设你是李华,你班计划于下周五晚上举行晚会,欢迎新来的交换生 Peter。请你给外籍教师 Mr. Black 写一封邀请函,邀请他一起参加欢迎会。

1. 提示词:dining hall, sing, dance, play games, make a welcome speech, gift.
2. 写作要点:(1)欢迎会的时间和地点;
　　　　　　(2)活动内容等。
3. 注意事项:(1)文中不得出现考生个人真实信息;
　　　　　　(2)词数80~100;
　　　　　　(3)开头和结尾已给出,不计入总词数。

Dear Mr. Black,

On behalf of our class, I'm writing to invite you to come to our welcome party.

_____
_____
_____
_____
_____
_____

Yours,

Li Hua

Grammar

一、从下面每小题四个选项中选出最佳选项

( ) 1. Tony and I _____ each other since last week. I don't know what he is doing these days.
   A. hasn't seen   B. haven't seen   C. don't see   D. doesn't see

( ) 2. Mary _____ the useful information, so she can't finish the work soon.
   A. won't find   B. doesn't find   C. hasn't found   D. didn't find

( ) 3. —Have you ever been to the Great Wall?
   —Yes, I _____ there last year.
   A. have been   B. have gone   C. go   D. went

( ) 4. —Mo Yan's new book _____. Let's go to buy one to read.
   —Good idea.
   A. will come out   B. has come out   C. had come out   D. would out

( ) 5. He came to the village in 2008, and he _____ the villagers a lot since then.
   A. helps   B. has helped   C. was helped   D. will help

( ) 6. Judy is a teacher of much experience, because she _____ English for 10 years.
   A. has taught   B. teaches   C. taught   D. will teach

( ) 7. —I _____ my dinner yet.
   —Hurry up! Our friends are waiting for us.
   A. hasn't finished   B. didn't finish   C. haven't finished   D. don't finish

( ) 8. As we all know, online learning _____ very popular with students for a few years.
   A. are becoming   B. has become   C. would become   D. had become

( ) 9. —Have you been in Jiangsu for a long time?
   —Yes, _____ the end of 2005.
   A. at   B. in   C. by   D. since

( ) 10. The Greens _____ in Fujian for seven years.
   A. have lived   B. has lived   C. would live   D. lives

( ) 11. Great changes _____ in our school since I worked here.
   A. has taken place   B. has happened
   C. have taken place   D. have happened

( ) 12. —Where is your sister?
　　　—She has _____ to Shanghai. She _____ back in a week.
　　　A. gone; will come　　　B. been; will come
　　　C. gone; has come　　　D. been; has come

( ) 13. The concert _____ since half an hour ago.
　　　A. has started　B. has ended　C. has been on　D. had been on

( ) 14. —How long can I _____ this book?
　　　—For two weeks.
　　　A. return　　B. keep　　C. buy　　D. borrow

( ) 15. Jane is productive and _____ five books in the past six years.
　　　A. wrote　　B. writes　　C. is writing　　D. has written

( ) 16. Jim _____ a lot about Chinese culture since he began to study in our school.
　　　A. learns　　B. learned　　C. has learned　　D. will learn

( ) 17. Mr. Yang isn't in the office. He _____ to the library.
　　　A. went　　B. goes　　C. has been　　D. has gone

( ) 18. I read a book written by Lu Xun yesterday and I _____ a lot from it.
　　　A. learn　　B. will learn　　C. have learned　　D. had learned

( ) 19. —It's a pity that there is no ticket for sale.
　　　—Don't worry. I _____ the tickets.
　　　A. am buying　　B. have bought　　C. will buy　　D. would buy

( ) 20. I _____ my keys. I have to wait here until my mother comes back.
　　　A. have lost　　B. will lose　　C. lose　　D. had lost

( ) 21. —Why do you know Canada so well?
　　　—Because I _____ there many times so far.
　　　A. have been to　B. have gone to　C. have been　D. have gone

( ) 22. He _____ his hometown for many years. Nearly no one knows him now.
　　　A. has been away from　　B. has left
　　　C. had been away from　　D. had left

( ) 23. The highway _____ for more than ten years.
　　　A. has opened　　B. has been open
　　　C. has been opened　　D. opened

( ) 24. The movie *Changjin Lake* is really a good one and I _____ it twice.
　　　A. see　　B. saw　　C. have seen　　D. would see

( ) 25. —When did your parents get married?

—In 1999. They _____ for over 20 years.

  A. have been married   B. have got married

  C. has been married   D. has got married

( )26. It's nice to see you again. We _____ each other for two months.

  A. didn't see   B. don't see   C. wouldn't see   D. haven't seen

( )27. We _____ good friends since we joined the same club.

  A. have become   B. has become   C. have been   D. has been

( )28. Jerry _____ whether to study abroad up to now.

  A. hasn't decided   B. hadn't decided   C. didn't decide   D. doesn't decide

( )29. My father has taught in this school _____ he was 22 years old.

  A. for   B. until   C. since   D. because

( )30. I joined the book club last month and I _____ two books already.

  A. am reading   B. will read   C. read   D. have read

二、根据要求转换句子

1. I have learned English since two years ago.（同义句转换）

  I have learned English _____.

2. The boss left five days because of his business.（同义句转换）

  The boss _____ for five days because of his business.

3. Tom has already finished the project on time.（改为否定句）

  Tom _____ finished the project on time.

4. Mike's mother has bought <u>a new bike</u> for him.（对划线部分提问）

  _____ Mike's mother bought for him?

5. Simon bought the computer two weeks ago.（同义句转换）

  Simon _____ the computer for two weeks.

6. I haven't heard from him yet.（改为肯定句）

  I _____ already _____ from him.

7. We have lived in the building <u>since five years ago</u>.（对划线部分提问）

  _____ have you lived in the new building?

8. The girl has finished reading the novel.（改为一般疑问句）

  _____ the girl _____ reading the novel?

9. Linda has never been to China.（改为反意疑问句）

  Linda has never been to China, _____?

10. The film began a few minutes ago.（同义句转换）

The film _____ for a few minutes.

For Better Performance

一、找出与所给单词画线部分读音相同的选项

( ) 1. att<u>e</u>nd   A. t<u>a</u>xi   B. <u>a</u>like   C. <u>a</u>ctive   D. m<u>a</u>nager

( ) 2. gr<u>ow</u>th   A. <u>ow</u>ner   B. fl<u>ow</u>er   C. p<u>ow</u>er   D. all<u>ow</u>

( ) 3. opportun<u>i</u>ty   A. sk<u>i</u>ll   B. d<u>i</u>scount   C. ed<u>i</u>tion   D. fam<u>i</u>ly

( ) 4. p<u>ar</u>tner   A. w<u>ar</u>m   B. popul<u>ar</u>   C. m<u>ar</u>keting   D. doll<u>ar</u>

( ) 5. supp<u>or</u>t   A. airp<u>or</u>t   B. neighb<u>or</u>   C. visit<u>or</u>   D. inf<u>or</u>mation

二、英汉互译

1. attend _____   2. 节拍 _____

3. celebrate _____   4. 典礼,仪式 _____

5. employee _____   6. 确认 _____

7. in common _____   8. 期待 _____

9. on behalf of _____   10. 发挥重要作用 _____

三、用括号内所给汉语提示或单词的适当形式填空

1. They had lunch in a _____ (自助餐厅).

2. The new book was the cultural _____ (重要事件) of the year.

3. We will _____ (invite) all our relatives to the wedding.

4. Mr. Brown is in charge of the _____ (market) in the company.

5. I will _____ (attendance) the meeting tomorrow morning.

6. The manager was called on to speak at the _____ (宴会).

7. The twin brothers have a lot in _____ (共同处).

8. The Panama Canal has played a very important _____ (角色) in transportation.

9. Speeches are made to praise outstanding _____ (employ).

10. The Chinese have _____ (celebrate) the Spring Festival for thousands of years.

四、找出下列句子中错误的选项,并改正过来

1. Robert <u>has spent</u> three days <u>to prepare</u> <u>for</u> the <u>coming</u> match.
                A   B   C   D

2. I hear that the boy's grandmother has died for nearly ten years.
          A   B   C   D

3. There are going to be a welcome party for the employees this Sunday.
            A   B   C   D

4. We want to take this opportunity to thank you and to celebrate our successful.
                 A   B   C   D

5. The purpose is to celebrate the past year's success and look forward to the next year.
               A   B   C   D

单元检测

第一部分　英语知识运用(共分三节,满分 40 分)

第一节　语音知识：从 A、B、C、D 四个选项中找出其画线部分与所给单词画线部分读音相同的选项。(共 5 分,每小题 1 分)

(　　) 1. banquet　　A. cafeteria　　B. beat　　C. training　　D. favorite

(　　) 2. celebrate　　A. collect　　B. common　　C. reception　　D. section

(　　) 3. employee　　A. ceremony　　B. event　　C. size　　D. special

(　　) 4. confirm　　A. opportunity　　B. online　　C. college　　D. original

(　　) 5. invite　　A. invitation　　B. exciting　　C. sincerely　　D. visit

第二节　词汇与语法知识：从 A、B、C、D 四个选项中选出可以填入空白处的最佳选项。(共 25 分,每小题 1 分)

(　　) 6. Our manager will _____ the meeting this weekend.
　　A. attend　　B. join　　C. take part in　　D. join in

(　　) 7. Economic _____ is expected to average 2% next year.
　　A. grow　　B. grew　　C. grown　　D. growth

(　　) 8. All telephone reservations have been _____ in writing.
　　A. confirm　　B. confirmed　　C. confirms　　D. confirming

(　　) 9. The boss will hold a welcome party for the new _____ this Sunday.
　　A. employ　　B. employer　　C. employee　　D. employment

(　　) 10. Mr. Li refused his friend's _____ because he is so busy.
　　A. intention　　B. invention　　C. information　　D. invitation

(　　) 11. The wedding _____ took more than two hours and all the people present were very happy.
　　A. ceremony　　B. harmony　　C. company　　D. opportunity

( )12. He sharpened his knife in _____ for carving the meat.
   A. population   B. pollution   C. preparation   D. protection

( )13. We have a lot of things _____ besides music.
   A. in need   B. in common   C. in trouble   D. in advance

( )14. _____ the students' union, I'm writing to invite you to give us a speech on Chinese history.
   A. In honor of   B. In case of   C. In search of   D. On behalf of

( )15. Mr. Smith didn't _____ the invitation from ABC Company.
   A. accept   B. accepted   C. receive   D. received

( )16. This is a great game to _____ everyone _____ each other.
   A. get; know   B. get; to know   C. make; to know   D. let; to know

( )17. We are looking forward to _____ you at this celebration.
   A. see   B. saw   C. seen   D. seeing

( )18. My uncle's support has _____ in my growth.
   A. played an important role   B. played a important role
   C. made an great difference   D. made a great difference

( )19. People enjoy parties to celebrate _____ moments in their lives.
   A. specially   B. special   C. specialty   D. especial

( )20. —We're opening a new shopping mall in Shenzhen next month.
   —_____.
   A. Don't worry   B. You're welcome
   C. Congratulations   D. Take it easy

( )21. It's common _____ companies _____ an annual meeting around the New Year.
   A. for; holding   B. for; to hold   C. of; holding   D. of; to hold

( )22. —Can you give us _____ for the party activities?
   —Of course. I know an interesting game for welcome parties.
   A. some ideas   B. any ideas
   C. some informations   D. any informations

( )23. Lucy and his parents _____ China for two years.
   A. has gone to   B. have gone to   C. has been in   D. have been in

( )24. We should _____ if the invited person can attend the event in advance.
   A. look for   B. look   C. find out   D. find

( )25. All the members should attend the meeting _____.

A. on business B. on time C. on show D. on vacation

( )26. —_____?

—It's called *We Are Ready*.

A. What is the game B. Can I help you

C. How is the weather D. How do you feel

( )27. There will be a class party _____ the New Year _____ December 31st.

A. for; in B. in; for C. for; on D. on; for

( )28. We have been business partners _____.

A. in five years B. since ten years ago

C. after five years D. ten years ago

( )29. We have _____ the house with a yard for three years.

A. lived B. bought C. kept D. got

( )30. — Have you _____ a welcome party before?

—Yes, I have.

A. gone to B. gone C. been D. been to

第三节 完形填空：阅读下面的短文，从所给的 A、B、C、D 四个选项中选出正确的答案。（共 10 分，每小题 1 分）

There are many traditional festivals in China. I like Spring Festival best. It is an __31__ festival in our country. People all over the country celebrate it. It is __32__ in January or February, and it is often cold at this time of __33__.

Before it comes, my parents usually __34__ new clothes ready for me. We also __35__ Spring Festival couplets（对联）and Chinese lanterns.

On Spring Festival Eve, all the family members __36__ home and have a big family dinner. When we enjoy the __37__, we give each other our best wishes for the coming year. After dinner, we __38__ the Spring Festival Gala on TV. We like to set off fireworks at night.

On the first day of Spring Festival, we __39__ our friends and relatives. Children can get lucky money __40__ their grandparents, parents, uncle and aunts. We all have a good time during the festival.

( )31. A. important B. noisy C. wonderful D. usual

( )32. A. never B. seldom C. always D. sometimes

( )33. A. day B. week C. month D. year

( )34. A. buy B. get C. borrow D. prepare

( )35. A. put up B. stay up C. turn up D. look up

( )36. A. leave B. left C. return D. returned

( )37. A. breakfast   B. song   C. film   D. meal
( )38. A. see   B. watch   C. look   D. observe
( )39. A. follow   B. miss   C. visit   D. wish
( )40. A. to   B. from   C. at   D. in

第二部分　篇章与词汇理解(共分三节,满分50分)

第一节　阅读理解:阅读下列短文,从每题所给A、B、C、D四个选项中选出最恰当的答案。(共30分,每小题2分)

A

All countries around the world have their ways to celebrate the coming year. Here are some unusual new year traditions around the world you must know.

In Canada, they have an unusual new year tradition known as the Polar Bear Swim. Peter Pantages started this event in 1920 in Vancouver when his friends jumped in the freezing waters of the English Bay. Now, it is held in many places. But why do they do that? Many participants say that it starts off their year right since the icy water clears their heads—a cleansing for the mind and soul.

At midnight, people go to the streets and dance to drum beats to welcome the New Year. The London Eye stands in bright colors for the fireworks show at midnight. For hours before the clock strikes 12, people come together to watch shows. The London Eye is lit up each year for New Year's celebrations.

On New Year's Eve in Venice, Italy, the most popular celebrations are setting off fireworks in the street and the fireworks displays are great ways to send off the old year and welcome the new one. As the clock strikes midnight, the boat parade(游行) begins. People often enjoy a glass of wine on the boat to celebrate the New Year.

In Thailand, they have the January New Year's celebration by exchanging gifts with friends and family members. Then they get together to enjoy a traditional New Year's Eve rice cake. Thai people also celebrate Songkran, or the Thai New Year in April. The first day in Bangkok, people often have a big water fight because they believe that water washes away bad luck. So throwing water is a sign of well-wishing and respect.

( )41. Peter Pantages started Polar Bear Swim in _____.
    A. 1920   B. 1930   C. 1940   D. 1902
( )42. The underlined word "participants" in Paragraph 2 means _____ in Chinese.
    A. 学习者。   B. 参与者。   C. 面试者。   D. 候选者。

( )43. People in _____ can enjoy the boat parade when they celebrate the New Year.
　　A. Vancouver, Canada　　　　B. London, Britain
　　C. Venice, Italy　　　　　　　D. Bangkok, Thailand

( )44. How did people in Thailand celebrate Thai New Year's Day in April?
　　A. They watch shows in the street.
　　B. They have a big water fight.
　　C. They often exchange gifts with others.
　　D. They often enjoy a glass of wine on the boat.

( )45. Which country isn't mentioned in the passage?
　　A. Canada.　　B. Britain.　　C. Italy.　　D. France.

B

Here are some fun ways to celebrate your birthday.

Explore(探索) a new place

Generally, people celebrate birthdays at home or at a reserved place. So, I think you should do something different this time. You can just find a few random(随机的) places around your city to visit and explore.

Celebrate with nature

If you want to do something unique(独特) that you haven't ever done before, then go for this one. Find a place that is close to nature, like a valley, riverside, mountains, desert, etc.

In my opinion, you can have a nice camp in this kind of places and celebrate your birthday in the most amazing way. This will be the best birthday present of your life.

Get yourself something new

When was the last time you bought yourself something new? If it has been many days, then this is the best time you can get yourself something new. For example, if you are planning to buy a car, then buy a car. By doing this you will make your birthday <u>memorable</u>.

I still remember when I became 18 my dad gave me a car on my birthday. I still remember that day not because I was 18 but because that day my dad gave me a car. So if no one gives you something unforgettable, then go ahead and get yourself a gift.

( )46. People usually celebrate birthdays _____.
　　A. at home or at a reserved place
　　B. near a valley, riverside or mountains
　　C. in the forest or at an expensive hotel
　　D. in a big city or at a beautiful place

( )47. The underlined word "memorable" in Paragraph 5 means _____.

A. lonely   B. unforgettable   C. boring   D. lucky

( )48. Which of the following is not True?

A. People may celebrate their birthdays with nature.

B. You can make your birthday memorable by buying something new.

C. You should buy something expensive on your birthday.

D. It's a good way to explore a new place to spend your birthday.

( )49. The writer got a car from his father when he was _____ years old.

A. 16   B. 17   C. 18   D. 19

( )50. The passage mainly talks about _____.

A. how to celebrate the New Year

B. the ways of celebrating Children's Day

C. what should be bought on birthdays

D. some fun ways to celebrate our birthday

C

When a baby is one year old, there is a fun activity. People call it "Zhuazhou". It is an activity on a baby's first birthday in China.

On that day, parents usually put a small table on the bed. On the table there are some books, pens, rulers, food, toys and so on. Then parents put their baby at the table and the baby can take anything on it.

If a baby takes a book, people will say he or she will be good at writing. If a baby girl takes a kitchen utensil(厨具), people will say she will be a good wife. When a baby takes a cake or a toy, people will say he or she will know how to have a good time in life.

For example, my father took a book from the table on his first birthday. After that, my grandfather called him "Wenhao". Now my father is a writer and he writes a lot of good books.

( )51. Parents have the activity "Zhuazhou" when their baby is _____.

A. one week old   B. one month old   C. one year old   D. three years old

( )52. The underlined word "it" in Paragraph 2 refers to _____.

A. the table   B. the baby   C. the end   D. the book

( )53. If a baby girl takes a kitchen utensil, people will say that _____.

A. he will be a good husband

B. she will be good at writing

C. she will know how to have a good time in life

D. she will be a good wife

( )54. Why did the writer's grandfather call the writer's father "Wenhao"?

A. Because his grandfather thought the name was interesting.

B. Because his father loved reading books very much.

C. Because his father took a book from the table on his first birthday.

D. Because his grandfather wanted his father to be a good son.

(   )55. What's the best title for the passage?

A. How to Be a Writer   B. An Activity—Zhuazhou

C. The Future Job of a Child   D. How to Celebrate a Baby's Birthday

第二节　词义搭配：从(B)栏中选出(A)栏单词的正确解释。(共10分，每小题1分)

(A)	(B)
( )56. attend	A. having no special distinction or quality
( )57. celebrate	B. a formal event performed on a special occasion
( )58. common	C. a possible chance
( )59. employee	D. aiding the cause or policy or interests of
( )60. invitation	E. be present at
( )61. opportunity	F. a request to participate or be present
( )62. partner	G. the state of having been made ready
( )63. preparation	H. have a celebration
( )64. support	I. a person who is a member of a partnership
( )65. ceremony	J. a worker who is hired to perform a job

第三节　补全对话：根据对话内容，从对话后的选项中选出能填入空白处的最佳选项。(共10分，每小题2分)

A：Hi, Li Mei! There are some traditional festivals in China. __66__

B：My favorite festival is the Lantern Festival.

A：__67__

B：It's on January 15th of the lunar calendar every year.

A：__68__

B：We watch the lantern show and answer riddle to celebrate the festival.

A：__69__

B：We eat sweet dumplings for good luck at the festival.

A：I see. __70__

B：You're welcome.

A. When is it?

B. What's your favorite festival?

C. Thank you for telling me so much.

D. What do you do to celebrate it?

E. What special food do you eat at the festival?

第三部分　语言技能应用(共分四节,满分 30 分)

第一节　单词拼写:根据下列句子及所给汉语注释写单词。(共 5 分,每小题 1 分)

71. Every member of the band must follow the _____(节拍).

72. Linda's marriage _____(仪式)took place in the church.

73. We have _____(共同的)topics to talk about.

74. Her letter _____(证实)everything.

75. We have made _____(准备)for the coming exam.

第二节　词形变换:用括号内单词的适当形式填空,将正确答案写在相应题号后的横线上。(共 5 分,每小题 1 分)

76. The number of the _____(attend)will run to 90.

77. People in the city held a great party to _____(celebration)their victory.

78. The _____(employ)was dismissed for laziness.

79. Their _____(grow)rate is quiet slow.

80. Nobody in the office received an _____(invite)to the party.

第三节　改错:从 A、B、C、D 四个画线处找出一处错误的选项填入相应题号后的括号内,并在横线上写出正确答案。(共 10 分,每小题 2 分)

81. Mary <u>is</u> not <u>at</u> home. She <u>has been to</u> an office party.
　　　A　　　B　　　　　C　　　D

82. <u>Writing</u> an <u>invite</u> is one of the first <u>jobs</u> when you <u>prepare for</u> an event.
　　A　　　　B　　　　　　　　　C　　　　　　　D

83. You should <u>make</u> sure <u>that</u> the invited person <u>know</u> the purpose <u>of</u> the event.
　　　　　　A　　　　B　　　　　　　　　　C　　　　　　　　D

84. The class party will be <u>hold</u> at 4:00 p.m. <u>on</u> December 30th <u>in</u> <u>our</u> classroom.
　　　　　　　　　　　　A　　　　　　　B　　　　　　　　C　　D

85. The Chinese <u>have</u> <u>celebrated</u> the Spring Festival <u>since</u> <u>thousands of</u> years.
　　　　　　　A　　　B　　　　　　　　　　　　C　　　D

第四节　书面表达。(共 10 分)

寒假临近,春节将至。你班将举办"传播传统文化,喜迎新春佳节"的联欢会,假设你是班长李明,请你给外籍教师 Mr. Smith 写一封邀请函,邀请他一起参加联欢会。

1. 提示词：traditional, music, dumplings, Beijing opera, confirm.
2. 写作要点：(1)联欢会的时间、地点、活动内容等；
            (2)需要做的准备。
3. 注意事项：(1)文中不得出现考生个人真实信息；
            (2)词数80~100；
            (3)开头和结尾已给出，不计入总词数。

Dear Mr. Smith,

On behalf of our class, I'm writing to invite you to come to our party to celebrate the Spring Festival.

_____

_____

_____

_____

_____

_____

Yours,
Li Ming

Unit 6

Food and Drinks

Warming up

一、句型汇总

1. I like / love chicken. 我喜欢鸡肉。
2. I'm a big chicken lover. 我是一个非常喜欢吃鸡肉的人。
3. I don't like chicken. 我不喜欢鸡肉。
4. I can't stand chicken. 我受不了鸡肉。
5. I hate chicken. 我讨厌鸡肉。

二、英汉互译

1. dumplings _____
2. 矿泉水_____
3. steak _____
4. 沙拉_____
5. pudding _____
6. 鸡肉_____
7. orange juice _____
8. 麻婆豆腐_____
9. sweet and sour fish _____
10. 辣的_____
11. salty _____
12. 酸的_____

Listening and Speaking

一、找出与所给单词画线部分读音相同的选项

（　　）1. order　　　A. ordinary　　B. actor　　　C. visitor　　　D. operator

（　　）2. medium　　A. prepare　　　B. offer　　　C. Chinese　　　D. bestselling

（　　）3. mineral　　A. direction　　B. convenient　C. beverage　　　D. celebrate

（　　）4. recommend　A. cell　　　　B. recycle　　C. ice　　　　　D. effect

（　　）5. specialty　 A. protect　　　B. especially　C. electricity　　D. college

二、从 B 栏中找出与 A 栏中相对应的答语

A	B
1. Are you ready to order? 2. What do you recommend? 3. Anything to drink? 4. Would anyone like to have some more Mapo Tofu? 5. How would you like your steak cooked, rare, medium or well-done?	A. Orange juice, please. B. Medium, please. C. No, it's too spicy. D. Some chicken, please. E. Mapo Tofu is our specialty.

三、用所给句子补全下面对话

（At the door）

A：Good morning, madam.　1　

B：Good morning. I have booked Table Seven.

A：　2　

（At the table）

A：May I take your order, please?

B：Can I have the vegetable salad?

A：Sure.　3　

B：Fried fish and mushroom soup.

A：OK.　4　

B：A glass of apple juice, please.

A:OK. __5__

> A. Anything else?
> B. Welcome to our restaurant!
> C. Would you like something to drink?
> D. This way, please.
> E. Wait a moment, please.

四、场景模拟

编写一组对话,和你的朋友谈论一家餐馆。

提示词汇:best, specialty, delicious, expensive, service, have a try.

_____

_____

_____

_____

_____

_____

Reading and Writing

一、用括号内所给汉语提示或单词的适当形式填空

1. You _____(点菜) the dishes and I will pay the bill.

2. I prefer my steak _____(半熟的).

3. I should _____(recommend) it as a useful reference book.

4. The _____(special) of this restaurant is its fish soup.

5. They sold 30 bottles of _____(矿物的) water in the afternoon.

6. Some _____(mushroom) are poisonous.

7. The hotel offers its guests with a wide _____(various) of amusements.

8. Lack of cash is a limiting _____(因素).

9. His _____(质量) of life has improved a lot since the operation.

10. Chinese _____(菜肴) is very different from European.

二、完形填空

Have you ever been to a buffet restaurant（自助餐厅）? You can eat as __1__ as you want for one low price at these places.

Sadly, many of these restaurants have closed in the US __2__ the COVID-19 pandemic. At buffet restaurants, people have to share one serving area when they get their __3__, which makes it easier for sickness to spread. But for a long time, they were quite __4__.

"Buffet" is the French word for sideboard—a piece of furniture that was used __5__ food and display serving dishes. The word was later used to describe a new dining concept（理念）serving __6__ from a wide selection of dishes, including soups, salads, and other dishes.

__7__ buffet restaurants in the US are "all you can eat"—that is, you pay one price and can go back to the buffet table for seconds, thirds, or even __8__. Chinese buffets are very common in the US. __9__ in the small town where I went to college, there were three different Chinese buffet restaurants. I would often go there with my friends on weekends. For kids like us who didn't have much money, the Chinese __10__ was a lifesaver. Maybe that's the reason why it attracts many kids there.

( ) 1. A. many   B. much   C. more   D. most
( ) 2. A. because of   B. as a result   C. so that   D. instead of
( ) 3. A. service   B. experiences   C. seats   D. food
( ) 4. A. cheap   B. expensive   C. popular   D. change
( ) 5. A. to serve   B. serving   C. serve   D. be served
( ) 6. A. itself   B. yourself   C. everyone   D. someone
( ) 7. A. Few   B. Any   C. Most   D. Lots
( ) 8. A. four   B. fourths   C. fourth   D. forty
( ) 9. A. But   B. Although   C. Unless   D. Even
( ) 10. A. buffet   B. food   C. dishes   D. restaurant

三、阅读理解

Ms. Qin's Home—Cooking Noodles

Welcome to Ms. Qin's Home—Cooking Noodles. We make our noodles in very traditional ways to keep the natural taste. The best materials are chosen for our food to keep your safety. The noodles in our restaurant are made by hand, which makes them very different from others'.

Noodles
Beef and onion　￥20 Mutton and cabbage　￥20 Beef and potato　￥15 Egg and tomato　￥12 Vegetable only　￥8
Dishes
Meat and vegetable salad　￥25 Vegetable salad　￥15
Drinks
Soda water　￥4 Coca-Coca　￥3 Sprite　￥3 Honey Green Tea　￥5

In addition: For every two bowls of beef and onion noodles or mutton and cabbage noodles, one can get two drinks for free. You can choose any of our drinks freely.

Business hour: 10:00 a.m. to 10:00 p.m. Open all year round, except the seven-day holiday during the Spring Festival.

Order line: 0371-55660066 (You need to pay ￥2 for packing, and your address should be within 5 km.)

(　　) 1. _____ makes Ms. Qin's Home—Cooking Noodles different.

　　A. The best materials it uses

　　B. The ways its noodles are made

　　C. The different kinds of noodles it has

　　D. The name that comes from its owner Ms. Qin

(　　) 2. If you are a beef lover, how many kinds of noodles can you choose?

　　A. Two.　　　　B. Three.　　　　C. Four.　　　　D. Five.

(　　) 3. You can order _____ if you want to get free drinks.

　　A. two bowls of egg and tomato noodles

　　B. a bowl of egg and tomato noodles

　　C. two bowls of beef and onion noodles

　　D. two bowls of vegetable only noodles

(　　)4. How much will you pay for two bowls of mutton and cabbage noodles, a bowl of beef and potato noodles, one Coca-Cola and one Honey Green tea?

  A. ￥45. B. ￥55. C. ￥68. D. ￥75.

(　　)5. We can find this poster in a _____.

  A. cinema B. library C. clothes shop D. restaurant

四、书面表达

假设你姑姑在西湖边有一家餐馆——Good Luck Restaurant,假期期间会有很多外国游客来西湖旅游。请你为姑姑的餐馆写一份英文介绍。

1. 提示词:across from, Dongpo Pork, Kung Pao Chicken, delicious, steamed bread, juice, specialty, West Lake Vinegar Fish.

2. 要点包括:(1)餐馆的地址;

    (2)菜品及价格。

3. 注意事项:(1)文中不得出现考生个人真实信息;

    (2)词数80~100;

    (3)开头已给出,不计入总词数。

Would you like to come to Good Luck Restaurant to have Chinese dishes?

_____

_____

_____

_____

_____

_____

Grammar

一、从下面每小题四个选项中选出最佳选项

(　　)1. There are 55 _____ in our school.

  A. woman teacher   B. women teachers

  C. woman teachers   D. women teacher

(　　)2. —_____?

—Just one spoon.

　A. How many sugar　　　　　　　B. How many sugars

　C. How much sugar　　　　　　　D. How much sugars

(　) 3. The teacher bought 50 _____ for his students to draw pictures.

　A. pieces of paper　　　　　　　B. pieces of papers

　C. piece of paper　　　　　　　D. piece of papers

(　) 4. You'd better have a good rest after _____ work.

　A. two day　　B. two days'　　C. two days　　D. two day's

(　) 5. Mr. White had two _____ and some _____ in the evening.

　A. bananas; breads　　　　　　B. banana; breads

　C. banana; bread　　　　　　　D. bananas; bread

(　) 6. There _____ lots of _____ in this book.

　A. are; information　　　　　　B. are; informations

　C. is; information　　　　　　　D. is; informations

(　) 7. The new bridge in our village is _____.

　A. 100 meters long　　　　　　B. 100 meter long

　C. 100 long meters　　　　　　D. 100 long meter

(　) 8. People can choose _____ they like in that shop.

　A. a piece furniture　　　　　　B. some furniture

　C. some furnitures　　　　　　　D. a furniture

(　) 9. We planted many _____ in our school last year.

　A. apples trees　　B. pears trees　　C. apple tree　　D. pear trees

(　) 10. There are many _____ and _____ in the park this morning.

　A. men; children　B. man; child　　C. men; child　　D. man; children

(　) 11. When I have some problems with my math, I usually ask my friend for some _____.

　A. suggestion　　B. idea　　　C. advice　　　D. point

(　) 12. They travelled with some _____ on their trip to Beijing.

　A. German　　B. Germen　　C. Germens　　D. Germans

(　) 13. There are 56 _____ in our country.

　A. people　　B. peoples　　C. person　　D. persons

(　) 14. We can see two _____ and one _____ on Tom's desk.

　A. book; box　　B. books; boxes　　C. books; box　　D. book; boxes

(　) 15. The movie named *A Little Red Flower* shows _____ for their children.

A. parents love   B. parents' love   C. parents loves   D. parents' loves

( )16. We have little _____ in the fridge. Let's go and buy some for breakfast.

A. tomato   B. potato   C. egg   D. milk

( )17. It's for us to drink _____ before going to bed every day.

A. two glass of milk   B. two glass of milks

C. a glass of milk   D. a glass of milks

( )18. I had so _____ to do last night, so I didn't have a good rest.

A. much homework   B. much homeworks

C. many homework   D. many homeworks

( )19. —What would you like to drink?

—_____, please. I'm very thirsty.

A. Two glass of water   B. Two glasses of water

C. Three bottle of beer   D. Three bottles of beer

( )20. She heard _____ news and told it to _____ old friend.

A. /; a   B. a piece of; a

C. a piece of; an   D. /; an

( )21. My father brushes his _____ at 6:30 every morning.

A. teeth   B. teethes   C. tooth   D. toothes

( )22. Please help _____ to some _____, my dear friends.

A. yourself; fish   B. yourselves; fish

C. yourselves; fishes   D. yourself; fishes

( )23. I hope that there will be less _____ in the future.

A. people   B. trees   C. pollution   D. countries

( )24. There are more than 100 _____ in my uncle's company.

A. work   B. works   C. worker   D. workers

( )25. The number of the volunteers in our school is 200 and two thirds of them are _____.

A. girl student   B. girl students   C. girls students   D. girls student

( )26. The shop sells _____ at a very low price on Sunday.

A. child   B. child's   C. children   D. children's

( )27. The _____ in the bag is for you. Have it please.

A. apples   B. bread   C. clothes   D. things

( )28. Mrs. Li and Mr. Wang are _____. I like them very much.

A. science teachers   B. sciences teacher

C. sciences teachers　　　　　　D. science teacher

(　　)29. I'd like to buy _____ for my grandparents.

A. two bags of orange　　　　　　B. two bag of orange

C. two bags of oranges　　　　　　D. two bag of oranges

(　　)30. —Can I help you?

— I'd like _____ for my sons.

A. two pair of shoes　　　　　　B. two pairs of shoe

C. two pairs of shoes　　　　　　D. two shoes

二、根据要求转换句子

1. This is Mary's photo.（改为复数形式）

   _____ are Mary's _____.

2. They have made much progress in Chinese this year.（对画线部分提问）

   _____ have they made in Chinese this year?

3. I want two cups of juice.（对画线部分提问）

   _____ cups of juice do you want?

4. The dictionary is on the desk.（改为复数形式）

   The _____ on the desk.

5. Jane's father and mother teach math.（改为同义句）

   Jane's _____ are math _____.

6. These are my notes.（改为同义句）

   These _____ mine.

7. Mr. Li owns the supermarket.（改为同义句）

   Mr. Li is the _____ of the _____.

8. I like English better than any other subject.（改为同义句）

   Of all the _____, I like _____ best.

9. There is only one sheep on the hill.（对画线部分提问）

   How many _____ there on the hill?

10. These are delicious tomatoes.（改为单数形式）

    This _____ a delicious _____.

For Better Performance

一、找出与所给单词画线部分读音相同的选项

( ) 1. c<u>ui</u>sine   A. d<u>i</u>scount   B. j<u>ea</u>ns   C. c<u>u</u>stomer   D. <u>i</u>nteresting

( ) 2. d<u>i</u>ning   A. f<u>i</u>t   B. trad<u>i</u>tional   C. w<u>i</u>sely   D. <u>i</u>nternship

( ) 3. f<u>a</u>ctor   A. <u>a</u>ffect   B. dist<u>a</u>nce   C. f<u>a</u>mous   D. pr<u>a</u>ctice

( ) 4. m<u>u</u>shroom   A. c<u>u</u>stomer   B. q<u>u</u>ality   C. introd<u>u</u>ce   D. comm<u>u</u>nicate

( ) 5. pr<u>o</u>per   A. c<u>o</u>nfirm   B. c<u>o</u>mmon   C. h<u>o</u>ld   D. n<u>o</u>tice

二、英汉互译

1. cozy _____
2. 用餐 _____
3. factor _____
4. （肉）五分熟的 _____
5. mushroom _____
6. 质量 _____
7. recommend _____
8. 不同种类 _____
9. various _____
10. 特色菜 _____
11. proper _____
12. 餐馆 _____
13. cuisine _____
14. 点菜 _____

三、用括号内所给汉语提示或单词的适当形式填空

1. We got a new table for the _____ (dine) room.
2. Each of us can _____ (contribution) to the future of the world.
3. He didn't pay much _____ (注意，留心) to his clothes.
4. Would you like your steak well-done or _____ (三分熟的)?
5. We should learn to shop online _____ (wise).
6. _____ (辣的) food doesn't agree with me.
7. When are you going to get a _____ (properly) job?
8. There are _____ (variety) ways of solving this problem.
9. We shall be _____ (enable) to deal with all kinds of problems.
10. Several cars are available within this price _____ (范围).

四、找出下列句子中错误的选项，并改正过来

1. I'd <u>like</u> the <u>tomato soup</u>, <u>fruits</u> salad and <u>a steak</u>.
       A   B   C   D

2. Before <u>eat</u> out, people <u>tend to</u> use <u>apps</u> <u>to choose</u> a restaurant.
          A   B   C   D

3. During weekends, we <u>might</u> be able <u>go</u> <u>a little</u> bit further <u>for</u> a good restaurant.
                     A   B   C   D

4. There <u>are</u> eight famous <u>cuisine</u> in China, <u>offering</u> various <u>choices</u>.
          A   B   C   D

5. People <u>with</u> different <u>backgrounds</u> may like <u>differently</u> <u>tastes</u>.
          A   B   C   D

单元检测

第一部分　英语知识运用(共分三节,满分40分)

第一节　语音知识:从 A、B、C、D 四个选项中找出其画线部分与所给单词画线部分读音相同的选项。(共5分,每小题1分)

( )1. mushr<u>oo</u>m　　A. t<u>oo</u>th　　B. childh<u>oo</u>d　　C. bamb<u>oo</u>　　D. sch<u>oo</u>l

( )2. qual<u>i</u>ty　　A. <u>i</u>ntroduce　　B. d<u>i</u>strict　　C. fam<u>i</u>ly　　D. un<u>i</u>que

( )3. v<u>a</u>riety　　A. <u>a</u>ddress　　B. p<u>a</u>rent　　C. <u>a</u>dd　　D. sn<u>a</u>ck

( )4. c<u>o</u>zy　　A. fav<u>o</u>rite　　B. p<u>o</u>litics　　C. f<u>o</u>reign　　D. n<u>o</u>tice

( )5. famou<u>s</u>　　A. traditional　　B. vocational　　C. hand<u>s</u>　　D. attend

第二节　词汇与语法知识:从 A、B、C、D 四个选项中选出可以填入空白处的最佳选项。(共25分,每小题1分)

( )6. —_____?

　　— It's soft and delicious.

　　A. What do you think of the dumplings

　　B. Can you tell me the way to the post office

　　C. What's wrong with you

　　D. How do you do

( )7. Good service may give you a better experience when _____ out.

　　A. eat　　　　B. ate　　　　C. eaten　　　　D. eating

( )8. Dear students, please _____ the notice I sent.

A. be afraid of　　　　　　　　B. make contributions to
C. pay attention to　　　　　　D. be crazy about

( ) 9. _____ a general rating of 4 or 5 stars, we may also consider other factors.

　　A. Apart from　　B. Except　　C. In addition　　D. Except for

( ) 10. Make a list of what you have to do, and put them _____ with the most important at the top.

　　A. in addition　　B. in case　　C. in order　　D. in danger

( ) 11. On weekdays, we usually _____ a restaurant within walking distance.

　　A. choice　　B. choose　　C. chose　　D. chosen

( ) 12. People _____ go to restaurants with a good rating.

　　A. tends to　　B. tends　　C. tend to　　D. tend

( ) 13. Guangdong Cuisine _____ a variety of cooking methods.

　　A. are famous as　　B. are famous for　　C. is famous as　　D. is famous for

( ) 14. —Can I take your order now?

　　—_____.

　　A. It's cloudy today

　　B. It's on sale this week

　　C. I'd like the tomato soup, fruit salad and a steak

　　D. I feel dizzy today

( ) 15. I try my best to keep myself at a _____ weight and keep healthy.

　　A. proper　　B. high　　C. practical　　D. fat

( ) 16. This shirt should be washed by hand, or it will be _____.

　　A. closed　　B. fixed　　C. ruined　　D. sold

( ) 17. —Would you like to try the fish? It's our _____.

　　— Yes. I'll have the potato soup and the fish.

　　A. special　　B. specially　　C. especially　　D. specialty

( ) 18. It was Zhang Zhongjing, an ancient Chinese doctor, _____ invented this kind of dumplings.

　　A. that　　B. whom　　C. who　　D. whose

( ) 19. We should eat more _____ because it's good for our health.

　　A. fruit　　B. pear　　C. vegetable　　D. potato

( ) 20. —Would you like to have _____ Mapo Tofu?

　　— No, it's too spicy.

　　A. some most　　B. some more　　C. many most　　D. many more

Unit 6　Food and Drinks

(　　)21. This tool can be used in _____ ways.

　　A. variety of　　B. a variety　　C. a variety of　　D. various of

(　　)22. Here is _____ advice for your coming English exam.

　　A. any　　B. some　　C. a　　D. many

(　　)23. There are four _____ and two _____ in Tom's class.

　　A. Chinese; Russians　　B. China; Russians

　　C. Chinese; Russian　　D. China; Russian

(　　)24. —Would you like something to drink?

　　—_____.

　　A. A steak, please　　B. I'd like a plate of dumplings

　　C. I want fruit salad　　D. A glass of orange juice, please

(　　)25. My friend and I choose a restaurant within five _____ walk during the noon break.

　　A. minute's　　B. minutes'　　C. minute　　D. minute'

(　　)26. My mother went to the supermarket to buy some _____ and _____ this morning.

　　A. potatos; tomatos　　B. potatoes; tomatoes

　　C. potatos; tomatoes　　D. potatoes; tomatos

(　　)27. We should choose the restaurant _____ because the environment contributes greatly to our dinning experience.

　　A. unwise　　B. unwisely　　C. wise　　D. wisely

(　　)28. The dumpling in this restaurant is _____ sweet yeast dough.

　　A. made of　　B. made from　　C. made in　　D. made into

(　　)29. —What are these?

　　— They are two _____ for cutting apples.

　　A. knife　　B. knifes　　C. knives　　D. the knife

(　　)30. We can eat _____ food in Friendship Restaurant.

> Friendship Restaurant
> 　　We have different kinds of Japanese food here. The food menu is in Japanese and Chinese.
> 　　Tel: 315-8886
> 　　Time: 11:30 a.m.-10:00 p.m.

　　A. French　　B. Chinese　　C. Japanese　　D. English

第三节　完形填空：阅读下面的短文,从所给的 **A、B、C、D** 四个选项中选出正确的答案。(共 10 分,每小题 1 分)

Dear Anna,

　　How's your summer vacation going? I'm having fun in Shanghai, China. I am sitting in a __31__ now. It is big and there are about 50 tables in it. I'm eating some tofu and a small bowl of mutton noodles __32__ carrots. I'm also drinking some black tea. I will __33__ 50 yuan for the meal. The dumplings here look good, and I will eat __34__ next time. The __35__ here is very good. The noodles and the tofu are delicious, and the vegetables are fresh, __36__ the tea isn't very good. There are also many __37__ of fruit ice-cream in the restaurant. The people in the restaurant use chopsticks to __38__ meals. I can't use them and I'm learning __39__ to use them. It is very interesting. I think it will take me a long time to finish the meal. I will go back to New York next week. See you __40__.

　　　　　　　　　　　　　　　　　　　　　　　　　　　　　　　Yours,
　　　　　　　　　　　　　　　　　　　　　　　　　　　　　　　Sally

(　　)31. A. school　　　　B. hotel　　　　C. restaurant　　　D. supermarket
(　　)32. A. with　　　　　B. in　　　　　　C. on　　　　　　D. of
(　　)33. A. take　　　　　B. cost　　　　　C. spend　　　　D. pay
(　　)34. A. it　　　　　　B. them　　　　　C. any　　　　　D. all
(　　)35. A. people　　　　B. show　　　　　C. food　　　　　D. music
(　　)36. A. but　　　　　B. however　　　　C. so　　　　　　D. because
(　　)37. A. ways　　　　　B. kinds　　　　　C. pairs　　　　D. sets
(　　)38. A. make　　　　　B. cut　　　　　　C. have　　　　　D. move
(　　)39. A. what　　　　　B. how　　　　　　C. where　　　　D. that
(　　)40. A. now　　　　　B. ago　　　　　　C. before　　　　D. soon

第二部分　篇章与词汇理解(共分三节,满分 50 分)

第一节　阅读理解：阅读下列短文,从每题所给的 **A、B、C、D** 四个选项中选出最恰当的答案。(共 30 分,每小题 2 分)

A

　　Hi, everyone! My name is Lin Tao. I come from the capital of China, but this year I live in Changsha, Hunan.

　　Now I'm having lunch in a very special restaurant with my good friend from Zhengzhou, Henan. Do you want to know how special it is? In this restaurant, there are only two kitchen helpers. But every day there are over 800 people coming to eat in it. That's because this restaurant has three robot cooks. The robots can cook very quickly. People can get their food in five minutes.

Li Zhiming is the inventor of the robot cooks and he is also the boss of the restaurant. He is over forty years old this year. He says, "In my city, such a big restaurant needs eight to ten cooks and kitchen helpers. But my restaurant is different."

Do you want to eat food made by robot cooks? Please come to this restaurant to have a try. I think you will like the food here. It is really delicious.

( )41. Lin Tao comes to the special restaurant to _____.
　　A. have lunch with his friend　　B. buy a robot
　　C. help in the kitchen　　D. meet the inventor of the robot cooks

( )42. The special restaurant is in _____.
　　A. Zhengzhou, Henan　　B. Changsha, Hunan
　　C. the capital of China　　D. Fuzhou, Fujian

( )43. How many kitchen helpers are there in the special restaurant?
　　A. Only one.　　B. Only two.　　C. Only three.　　D. Only four.

( )44. What can we learn form the passage?
　　A. Lin Tao comes to the restaurant in the evening.
　　B. There are many people working in the restaurant.
　　C. The inventor of the robot cooks is 55 years old.
　　D. Many people come to eat in the restaurant every day.

( )45. What's the best title of the passage?
　　A. A special cook.　　B. A good friend.
　　C. A special restaurant.　　D. A smart robot.

B

When your parents are busy at work and have no time to cook, you can pick up the phone, order some food for yourself and the food will arrive at your home soon. Lots of people <u>order</u> takeout food these days. But did Chinese people eat takeout in the past?

The answer is yes! There was takeout as far back as the Song Dynasty (960-1279). People at that time didn't have phones, but they could still order food. According to history books, Emperor Xiaozong (宋孝宗) (1127-1194) liked to order takeout late at night. His servants then went around the city to pick up the dishes and bring them back.

Common people also liked to order takeout. Restaurant workers walked around the city or waited outside of theaters. They shouted loudly which dishes could be ordered that day. People paid them and then the workers would send food to their homes.

People at that time even had special meal boxes for take out dishes. It was a long wooden box with two layers(层). People put hot water between the two layers. In this way the dish could still keep warm when it arrived at people's home.

In the famous Song Dynasty painting *Along the River During the Qingming Festival*《清明上河图》, a takeout worker can be seen on the way to send food.

( )46. The underlined word "order" in Paragraph1 means _____.

  A. 顺序 B. 订单 C. 点(酒菜等) D. 条理

( )47. Emperor Xiaozong got his takeout by _____.

  A. picking up the dishes B. sending his servants

  C. walking around the city D. bringing takeout back

( )48. We can learn from the passage that in the Song Dynasty _____.

  A. takeout food was popular with people

  B. Emperor Xiaozong was the first one to order takeout

  C. only rich people could order takeout

  D. people paid for their takeout after they got it

( )49. The writer mentions the painting *Along the River During the Qingming Festival* in the last paragraph to show _____.

  A. why most people liked to order takeout

  B. that the painter was good at drawing

  C. that takeout started a long time ago

  D. how people ordered takeout at that time

( )50. The purpose of this passage is to _____.

  A. advise people to order takeout B. tell us the advantages of takeout

  C. remind us not to order takeout D. introduce takeout in the past

C

A student's kindness paid off. He received 5,000 yuan after ordering some take-out food for a homeless man.

Wang Ya is a university student in Kunming. One night, in the heavy rain, Wang saw a homeless man sleeping under a bridge wearing his summer clothes. Wang felt sorry for him, so he went online and ordered him some food. Wang also left a message for the restaurant. It said, "Please make sure that the homeless man gets the food as soon as possible. It's cold outside and I don't know if he has had anything to eat. I've seen him there since about 11:30 at noon." The restaurant owner was so moved that he added some food to the order. The homeless man got the food less than half an hour later.

Wang's story got so popular online that a charitable foundation(慈善基金会)gave him 5,000 yuan for his kindness. But he refused to spend the money on himself and he gave it to charities.

(　　)51. What was the weather like when Wang noticed the homeless man?
　　　　　A. Cloudy.　　　B. Windy.　　　C. Rainy.　　　D. Snowy.

(　　)52. Wang ordered food for the homeless man because _____.
　　　　　A. the man asked him to do so　　　B. he felt sorry for the man
　　　　　C. he wanted to be popular　　　　D. he wanted to make money

(　　)53. We can infer the man slept _____.
　　　　　A. under the bridge　　　　　B. in his home
　　　　　C. in the school　　　　　　D. in the hotel

(　　)54. Which of the following is Not true according to the passage?
　　　　　A. The restaurant owner added some food to the order.
　　　　　B. The homeless man got the takeout food in the end.
　　　　　C. A charitable foundation gave Wang 5,000 yuan.
　　　　　D. Wang took the money to buy clothes for homeless people.

(　　)55. In which part of a newspaper can we read the passage?
　　　　　A. Music.　　　B. History.　　　C. Life.　　　D. Science.

第二节　词义搭配：从(B)栏中选出(A)栏单词的正确解释。(共10分,每小题1分)

　　　　(A)　　　　　　　　　　　　　(B)

(　　)56. dinning　　　　　　A. widely known
(　　)57. environment　　　　B. the act of eating dinner
(　　)58. factor　　　　　　　C. express a good opinion of
(　　)59. famous　　　　　　D. a building where people go to eat
(　　)60. proper　　　　　　　E. showing or resulting from lack of wisdom
(　　)61. recommend　　　　F. the area in which something exists or lives
(　　)62. restaurant　　　　　G. destroy completely
(　　)63. ruin　　　　　　　　H. having all the qualities typical of the thing specified
(　　)64. unwise　　　　　　　I. of many different kinds
(　　)65. various　　　　　　　J. anything that contributes causally to a result

第三节　补全对话：根据对话内容,从对话后的选项中选出能填入空白处的最佳选项。(共10分,每小题2分)

A: Welcome! This way, please.
B: ___66___
A: Here is a table by the window. Is it OK for you?

B：OK. I'll take that table.

A： __67__ Here is the menu.

(A few minutes later.)

A： __68__

B：Sure. I'd like Italian pizza.

A： __69__ We have different kinds of juice.

B：Let me see. I'll have a bottle of orange juice.

A： __70__

B：That's enough.

A：OK, wait a moment, please.

> A. Sit down, please.
> B. Would you like something to drink?
> C. Thank you.
> D. Anything else?
> E. May I take your order?

第三部分　语言技能应用(共分四节,满分 30 分)

第一节　单词拼写:根据下列句子及所给汉语注释写单词(共 5 分,每小题 1 分)

71. She is not used to the new _____(环境).

72. New York is _____(著名的)for its skyscrapers.

73. He could not come up with a _____(合适的)answer.

74. Can you _____(推荐)me some new books on this subject?

75. The _____(餐馆)gets three stars in the guidebook.

第二节　词形变换:用括号内单词的适当形式填空,将正确答案写在相应题号后的横线上。(共 5 分,每小题 1 分)

76. I gathered many _____(mushroom) after rain.

77. I have _____(order) chicken and chips for you.

78. The rain _____(ruin) my painting last month.

79. What's the _____(special) in your restaurant?

80. It is _____(wise) to swim on a full stomach.

第三节　改错:从 A、B、C、D 四个画线处找出一处错误的选项填入相应题号后的括号内,并在横线上写出正确答案。(共 10 分,每小题 2 分)

81. We should <u>choice</u> a restaurant <u>within</u> a <u>proper</u> price <u>range</u>.
　　　　　　　A　　　　　　　　　B　　　　C　　　　D

82. <u>Spending</u> too <u>many</u> money in <u>eating</u> <u>is</u> unwise.
        A   B   C   D

83. The environment <u>of</u> a restaurant <u>contribute</u> <u>greatly</u> <u>to</u> your dining experience.
                  A   B   C D

84. There <u>are</u> <u>many</u> <u>difference</u> cultures <u>in</u> the world.
         A   B   C   D

85. Jiaozi <u>has</u> many different <u>flavors</u>, <u>depend</u> on <u>what</u> you put inside.
          A   B   C   D

第四节　书面表达。(共10分)

你班的国际交换生Peter想在本周末品尝一下中国美食。假设你是李华，请给Peter写一封邮件，向他推荐一家北京的餐馆，并说明理由。

1. 提示词：close, delicious, large, fresh, reasonable, service.
2. 写作要点：(1)餐馆特点；
   (2)推荐的特色菜。
3. 注意事项：(1)文中不得出现考生个人真实信息；
   (2)词数80~100；
   (3)开头和结尾已给出，不计入总词数。

Dear Peter,

I hear that you plan to choose a restaurant to taste the local food this weekend.

_____
_____
_____
_____
_____
_____
_____

I hope you can enjoy yourself there.

                                                  Yours,
                                                Li Hua

Unit 7

The Internet

Warming up

一、句型总结

1. Could you spare me a few minutes? 您能抽出几分钟时间吗?

2. Have you ever played games online? 您玩过网络游戏吗?

3. What made you stop playing those games? 是什么让您不再玩那些游戏了?

4. It's really wise to quit before it's too late. 及时戒除是明智的。

5. I often stayed up so late playing games that I couldn't even concentrate on my studies. 我过去经常熬夜玩游戏,以至于不能集中精力学习。

6. With smartphones, the Internet becomes mobile, and we can do most of the things we do on a typical day without moving around much. 有了智能手机,互联网变得可以移动,我们不用四处奔走就可以完成日常生活中的大部分事情。

7. It's sent to you at your desired time. 它在你期望的时间送达。

8. It's said that... 据说……

9. It's necessary to make cities smarter. 我们有必要让城市变得更智慧。

10. Life in a smart city could be much safer, greener and more convenient. 智慧城市中的生活可以更安全、更绿色、更便利。

二、英汉互译

1. click _____   2. desired _____

3. icon _____   4. selfie _____
5. take-out _____   6. 路人 n._____
7. 流行的,受欢迎的 adj. _____   8. 抽出,节约 v._____
9. 典型的, 有代表性的 adj. _____   10. 采访 v._____
11. 专心…… _____   12. 复习,重温_____
13. 使用,接近_____   14. 登录,进入_____
15. 熬夜_____

Listening and Speaking

一、找出与所给单词画线部分读音相同的选项

(   ) 1. popular   A. up   B. much   C. unlock   D. music
(   ) 2. icon   A. cozy   B. done   C. cotton   D. convenience
(   ) 3. typical   A. yellow   B. yard   C. why   D. spicy
(   ) 4. accept   A. according B. accounting C. access   D. account
(   ) 5. think   A. send   B. ruin   C. bank   D. tend

二、从 B 栏中找出与 A 栏中相对应的答语

A

1. Thank you for your time.
2. How often did you share your selfies online?
3. Have you ever had classes online?
4. How much time do you spend online every day?
5. How much is it?

B

A. Almost every day.
B. It's about 200 yuan.
C. About two hours.
D. Sure.
E. You are welcome.

三、用所给句子补全下面对话

A：Excuse me, I'm doing a survey about online activities. Could you spare a few minutes?

B：__1__. What would you like to ask?

A：Have you ever shared selfies online?

B：Sure. __2__.

A：How often did you share your selfies online?

B：___3___.

A：Why did you like sharing selfies online?

B：___4___. We had a lot to share with friends.

A：OK. Thanks for your time.

B：___5___.

> A. I used to share a lot of selfies online, but not anymore
> B. OK
> C. It was quite popular among young people
> D. You are welcome
> E. Almost every day

四、场景模拟(主题对话)

假设教育部门正在开展学生上网课(have classes online)情况调查，编写一组对话。

提示：Have you ever…?

　　　Why did you like doing…?

_____
_____
_____
_____
_____
_____

Reading and Writing

一、用括号内所给汉语提示或单词的适当形式填空

1. Smartphones makes our life more _____(便利).

2. We can do most of the things we do on a _____ (典型的) day without moving around much.

3. The teacher is talking about _____(诗).

4. You log onto a _____(外卖的) app.

5. It's one of my _____（最喜爱的）movies.

6. We should eat plenty of _____（新鲜的）fruit and vegetables.

7. You can _____（分享）sorrows and joys with your close friends.

8. Please tell us your _____（经历）in America.

9. He offered us a lot of _____（信息）on climate.

10. I feel _____（舒服的）to live in a big room.

二、完形填空

The Internet has become an important part of teenage life. Most of them use the Internet to get lots of knowledge and __1__. The teenagers keep in touch with their friends online. It's __2__ than phoning someone far away and e-mail is __3__ much quicker than ordinary mail. But some teenagers are not using it __4__ the right way.

Some of them would find life difficult without it. Some teenagers spend __5__ time online. Some of the students who used to do well at school are now failing in exams because now they spend most of their __6__ playing games online. It is __7__ for teenagers to use the Internet properly. They should learn __8__ to use the Internet for study and keep away from __9__ websites. They should make sure that surfing the Net doesn't __10__ their homework or being with their friends.

( ) 1. A. discussions   B. friends   C. information   D. money

( ) 2. A. more expensive   B. dearer   C. cheapest   D. cheaper

( ) 3. A. too   B. also   C. either   D. as well

( ) 4. A. in   B. by   C. with   D. on

( ) 5. A. much too   B. too much   C. too many   D. so many

( ) 6. A. time   B. money   C. knowledge   D. attention

( ) 7. A. useless   B. important   C. impossible   D. unpleasant

( ) 8. A. what   B. why   C. where   D. how

( ) 9. A. good   B. useful   C. bad   D. healthy

( ) 10. A. take the place of   B. take place   C. take down   D. take off

三、阅读理解

When can I get a cell phone? The answer is when your parents think you need one, though many kids seem to be getting them around age 12 or 13. Some younger kids may have them because their parents see it as a matter of safety and convenience. For example, a kid can call mom and dad when sports practice is over. And a cell phone can give kids almost instant access(快捷通道) to their parents if something goes wrong or they need help. It can give parents quick access to their kids so they can check on them and make sure they're OK.

If you do get a cell phone, make some rules with your parents, such as how many minutes you're allowed to spend on the phone, when you can use your phone, when the phone must be turned off, and what you will do if someone calls you too often, and so on.

You also have to learn to take care of the phone in your life. Keep it charged(充电) and store it in the safe place so it does not get lost. And whatever you do, don't use it in the bathroom. I know someone who dropped her phone in the toilet!

( ) 1. Parents buy cell phones for their kids because _____.

  A. they think it is necessary

  B. they think their kids are old enough

  C. they have asked the author for advice

  D. they want to follow their kids wherever they are

( ) 2. The author of the passage _____.

  A. wants to describe how children use cell phones

  B. knows nothing about when children can have a cell phone

  C. may have done a survey on kids using cell phones

  D. has been a teacher for many years

( ) 3. Which of the following is true?

  A. It is too young for kids of 12 or 13 to get a cell phone.

  B. A cell phone is useful for kids and their parents.

  C. The author is against the idea of kids to have cell phones.

  D. Most kids are considering having cell phones.

( ) 4. Who is the passage most probably written by?

  A. Parents who have bought phones for their kids.

  B. Someone who does cell phone business.

  C. A teacher who cares most about school safety.

  D. Someone who works for children's education.

( ) 5. Which might not be a rule for kids with a cell phone?

  A. Keep it on all the time.

  B. Make a call if something goes wrong.

  C. Don't use it in the bathroom.

  D. Take care not to lose it.

四、书页表达

作文题目：Talking about Exploring the Internet

词数要求：80~100 词

写作要点：(1) 上网可以让我们很快地了解国内外新闻，使人们的生活更方便：购物、看病、学习、发电子邮件等；

(2) 网上的一些不健康的内容或游戏等对学生产生了很坏的影响；

(3) 我们应该很好地利用网络。

_____
_____
_____
_____
_____
_____
_____

Grammar

一、从下面每小题四个选项中选出最佳选项

( ) 1. The twins _____ the clothes now.
　　A. is washing　　B. are washing　　C. wash　　D. were washing

( ) 2. Look! He _____ basketball over there.
　　A. is playing　　B. plays　　C. was playing　　D. played

( ) 3. It is 6:00. The Smiths _____ supper.
　　A. have　　B. has　　C. is having　　D. are having

( ) 4. Don't make so much noise. The students _____ an English exam.
　　A. are taking　　B. were taking　　C. take　　D. took

( ) 5. Listen! They _____ songs for the 100 birthday of the CCYL(中国共青团).
　　A. are singing　　B. sang　　C. will sing　　D. is singing

( ) 6. — Where's Anna, dear?
　　— She _____ an online class in her room.
　　A. is taking　　B. takes　　C. will take　　D. would take

(　　) 7. —Nanjing Road is very crowded these days.
—The workers _____ it. It is said that it _____ soon.
A. repair; finishes   B. have repaired; will finish
C. are repairing; will be finished   D. repaired; finished

(　　) 8. — Is your father at home, Jill?
— No. He _____ his car outside.
A. was washing   B. will wash   C. is washing   D. washed

(　　) 9. The workers _____ the community center now.
A. cleaned   B. were cleaning   C. will clean   D. are cleaning

(　　) 10. Holly prefers playing the piano to _____ the violin. Listen! She _____ the piano in her room.
A. play; is playing   B. playing; plays
C. playing; is playing   D. play; plays

(　　) 11. —Why is Kate absent from class?
—Oh, she _____ the meeting.
A. was attending   B. attended   C. is attending   D. attends

(　　) 12. —Hello! May I speak to Kate?
—Sorry, she isn't in. She _____ ping-pong outside.
A. is playing   B. plays   C. played   D. will play

(　　) 13. —Paul, where's your mom?
—She _____ for us in the kitchen now.
A. will cook   B. cooks   C. is cooking   D. cooked

(　　) 14. — Be quiet. I'm on the phone.
—Who _____ you _____ to, mom?
A. do; speak   B. are; speaking   C. will; speak   D. have; spoken

(　　) 15. — Excuse me, what is Nick doing?
— Look! He _____ flowers outside.
A. waters   B. watered   C. is watering   D. has watered

(　　) 16. —Here comes the bus. Is everyone here?
—No. Sam _____ a meeting in the school hall now.
A. have   B. had   C. will have   D. is having

(　　) 17. —Listen! Amy, who _____ next door?
—Well, it's Cindy. Her voice always sounds _____ just like a bird.
A. sings; sweetly   B. is singing; sweet

Unit 7 The Internet

C. sings; sweet   D. is singing; sweetly

(   )18. The headmaster is not available now. He _____ to the new teachers.
      A. speaks   B. spoke   C. is speaking   D. was speaking

(   )19. —The classroom is so quiet.
      —Yes, all the students _____ for the final exam.
      A. prepare   B. prepared   C. will prepare   D. are preparing

(   )20. Students in Class One _____ for the singing competition at the moment.
      A. prepare   B. are preparing
      C. prepared   D. are going to prepare

(   )21. Look! Julia as well as her sisters _____ a kite on the playground.
      A. fly   B. flies   C. is flying   D. are flying

(   )22. Look! The musician _____ at the piano, ready to play.
      A. sat   B. will sit   C. is sitting   D. was sitting

(   )23. —Don't make noise! The children _____ online.
      —Sorry, I won't.
      A. studies   B. are studying   C. studied   D. were studying

(   )24. —The policewoman _____ the driver for breaking the traffic rules.
      —That's right. He's explaining to her loudly over there.
      A. is punishing   B. was punishing   C. would punish   D. is punished

(   )25. —What's the weather like today?
      —It's a _____ day. It's _____ heavily now.
      A. raining; rainy   B. rainy; raining   C. rainy; rainy   D. raining; raining

(   )26. —Peter, what are you doing?
      —Oh, I _____ a report about national heroes.
      A. will write   B. am writing   C. wrote   D. have written

(   )27. —Where is mum?
      —In the living room. She _____ a book at the moment.
      A. was reading   B. will read   C. is reading   D. has read

(   )28. Listen! Our science teacher _____ the use of the robot.
      A. explains   B. explained   C. is explaining   D. has explained

(   )29. —What is Jane doing these days?
      —She _____ a book about the history of the People's Republic of China.
      A. reads   B. has read   C. is reading   D. read

(   )30. It _____ dark. Shall I turn on the light?

A. gets   B. got   C. is getting   D. was getting

二、找出下列句子中错误的选项,并改正过来

1. What is your father do now?
   A   B   C D
2. My brother as well as his friends are playing football on the playground.
                        A   B   C   D
3. My mother and my sister is watching TV in the living room at this moment.
                           A   B   C   D
4. Listen! She is sing in the next room.
   A   B   C   D
5. My brother is plays the guitar now.
   A   B C   D

For Better Performance

一、找出与所给单词画线部分读音相同的选项

(   ) 1. cl<u>i</u>ck   A. w<u>i</u>se   B. ch<u>i</u>ld   C. b<u>i</u>ll   D. m<u>o</u>bile
(   ) 2. c<u>o</u>ncentrate A. c<u>o</u>ntribute B. c<u>o</u>ntribution C. c<u>o</u>nfirm   D. c<u>o</u>nvenient
(   ) 3. unl<u>o</u>ck   A. l<u>o</u>g   B. <u>o</u>pen   C. ph<u>o</u>to   D. v<u>o</u>cational
(   ) 4. popul<u>a</u>r   A. f<u>a</u>r   B. l<u>a</u>rge   C. p<u>a</u>rtner   D. gr<u>a</u>mmar
(   ) 5. <u>ou</u>t   A. en<u>ou</u>gh   B. s<u>ou</u>nd   C. t<u>ou</u>ch   D. c<u>ou</u>ld

二、英汉互译

1. fresh (adj.) ＿＿＿＿＿＿   2. ring (v.) ＿＿＿＿＿＿
3. mobile (adj.) ＿＿＿＿＿＿   4. poem (n.) ＿＿＿＿＿＿
5. survey (n.) ＿＿＿＿＿＿   6. used to ＿＿＿＿＿＿
7. 舒适的 (adj.) ＿＿＿＿＿＿   8. 必要的 (adj.) ＿＿＿＿＿＿
9. 人口 (n.) ＿＿＿＿＿＿   10. 智能手机 (n.) ＿＿＿＿＿＿

三、用括号内所给汉语提示或单词的适当形式填空

1. He often stays up late ＿＿＿＿＿ (play) games.
2. What made you stop ＿＿＿＿＿ (play) those games?
3. Why did you like ＿＿＿＿＿ (play) games online?

4. The student listened to the teacher _____ (careful).

5. It is sent to you at your _____ (desire) time.

6. We are now "_____ (depend) on" our mobile phones.

7. Here is a list of _____ (suggest) about English study.

8. He is much _____ (tall) than his brother.

9. Listen! Those girls are _____ (sing) songs.

10. She kept _____ (silence), saying nothing.

四、找出下列句子中错误的选项，并改正过来

1. Look! What are the boys do over there?
          A   B   C   D

2. Life in a smart city could be more safer, greener and more convenient.
     A   B   C   D

3. The phone is ring for morning hobby classes at eight.
             A   B   C   D

4. You can't depend at your mobile phone to discuss things with your partners.
            A   B   C   D

5. After send homework to your teacher by email, you decide to have some fun.
       A   B   C   D

单元检测

第一部分　英语知识运用

第一节　语音知识：从 A、B、C、D 四个选项中找出其画线部分与所给单词画线部分读音相同的选项。（共 5 分，每小题 1 分）

(　　) 1. cook　　A. food　　B. school　　C. cool　　D. wood

(　　) 2. go　　A. cover　　B. hope　　C. come　　D. stop

(　　) 3. put　　A. solution　　B. blue　　C. ruler　　D. push

(　　) 4. learn　　A. earth　　B. dear　　C. clear　　D. wear

(　　) 5. safe　　A. rose　　B. season　　C. past　　D. busy

第二节　词汇与语法知识：从 A、B、C、D 四个选项中选出可以填入空白处的最佳选项。（共 25 分，每小题 1 分）

(　　) 6. Jenny likes playing _____ piano while Mike likes playing _____ football.
       A. the; the　　B. /; /　　C. /; the　　D. the; /

(   )7. I like to _____ white shirts in summer.
   A. dress   B. wear   C. put on   D. take off

(   )8. My son is old enough to _____ himself.
   A. dress   B. wear   C. put on   D. take off

(   )9. He _____ his new pair of sunglasses and went out.
   A. dress   B. wear   C. put on   D. take off

(   )10. My son can't go to the cinema with you. He must _____ the lessons first.
   A. go on   B. go over   C. go down   D. go into

(   )11. He _____ in a small village, but now he _____ in a big city.
   A. used to live; is used to live
   B. is used to live, is used to living
   C. is used to living; used to living
   D. used to live; is used to living

(   )12. Mike _____ after dinner, but now he quit it.
   A. is used to smoke   B. is used to smoking
   C. used to smoke   D. used to smoking

(   )13. He often stay up late _____ computer games.
   A. playing   B. plays   C. played   D. play

(   )14. The teacher is popular _____ students.
   A. at   B. in   C. with   D. to

(   )15. She enjoys _____ piano.
   A. to play the   B. playing the   C. to play   D. playing

(   )16. —What a good _____ you've given me! Thanks a lot.
   —My pleasure.
   A. information   B. news   C. suggestion   D. advice

(   )17. They are building houses now. There is not _____ money for them.
   A. too many   B. too much   C. many too   D. much too

(   )18. He _____ too much time chatting online.
   A. spent   B. cost   C. paid   D. took

(   )19. It _____ me two hours to do my homework yesterday.
   A. took   B. spent   C. cost   D. paid

(   )20. It _____ us about a day to finish the work.
   A. spent   B. cost   C. paid   D. took

(   )21. Did you spend _____ hour _____ your homework?
   A. an; do   B. an; did   C. a; do   D. an; doing

(   )22. I would like _____ basketball after school.

A. play　　　　B. to play　　　　C. playing　　　　D. to playing

(　)23. Mary, together with her parents,_____ to see us off tonight.

A. are coming　　B. is coming　　C. comes　　D. come

(　)24. What made you _____ the work so quickly?

A. finish　　B. finished　　C. to finish　　D. finishing

(　)25. Are you _____ for Beijing tomorrow?

A. leave　　B. leaving　　C. to leave　　D. left

(　)26. _____ is very difficult to choose where to live.

A. This　　B. That　　C. It　　D. One

(　)27. I shared my lunch _____ him.

A. with　　B. of　　C. in　　D. between

(　)28. —Thanks for the lovely party and the delicious food.

—_____.

A. Never mind　　B. All right　　C. With pleasure　　D. My pleasure

(　)29. Finally, he _____ a good idea.

A. come up　　B. came up　　C. come up with　　D. came up with

(　)30. He drove away without _____ good-bye.

A. say　　B. said　　C. saying　　D. to say

第三节　完形填空:阅读下面的短文,从所给的 A、B、C、D 四个选项中选出正确的答案。(共10分,每小题1分)

These days computer games have become more and more popular in many cities and towns. A lot of small shops along busy street have changed into computer game houses in order to get more __31__. These places are always crowded with people. In the computer game houses, people __32__ a lot of money matching on the machines. People want to __33__ when they play computer games. The more they play, the more they want to win, and at last they even can't __34__ without it.

The result is that some people don't want to __35__ and they play in computer game houses for hours and hours. For schoolboys, things are even __36__. They don't want to have __37__. When school is over, they rush to the computer game houses near their schools. Some of them can get enough money from their __38__. Some of them are not __39__ enough to get the money. So they have to steal or rob(盗窃或抢劫) others' and become bad.

Computer game addiction is a(n) __40__ problem in our lives. Something has to be done to stop it.

(　)31. A. boys　　B. money　　C. computers　　D. houses

(   )32. A. take   B. spend   C. pay   D. cost
(   )33. A. lose   B. do   C. win   D. get
(   )34. A. live   B. eat   C. study   D. play
(   )35. A. sleep   B. eat   C. work   D. help
(   )36. A. better   B. harder   C. worse   D. less
(   )37. A. lessons   B. games   C. sports   D. computers
(   )38. A. classmates B. teachers   C. friends   D. parents
(   )39. A. clever   B. lucky   C. careful   D. good
(   )40. A. important B. serious   C. unusual   D. crazy

第二部分　篇章与词汇理解

第一节　阅读理解：阅读下面的短文，从每题所给的 A、B、C、D 四个选项中选出最恰当的答案。(共 30 分，每小题 2 分)

A

Perhaps you have heard a lot about the Internet, but what is it, do you know? The Internet is a network. It uses the telephone to join millions of computers together around the world.

Maybe that doesn't sound very interesting. But when you've joined to the Internet, there are lots and lots of things you can do. You can send e-mails to your friends, and they can get them in a few seconds. You can also do with all kinds of information on the World Wide Web (WWW).

There are many different kinds of computers now. They all can be joined to the Internet. Most of them are small machines sitting on people's desks at home, but there are still many others in schools, offices or large companies. These computers are owned by people and companies, but no one really owns the Internet itself.

There are lots of places for you to go into the Internet. For example, your school may have the Internet. You can use it during lessons or free time. Libraries often have computers joined to the Internet. You are welcome to use it at only time.

Thanks to the Internet, the world is becoming smaller and smaller. It is possible for you to work at home with a computer in front, getting and sending the information you need. You can buy or sell whatever you want by the Internet. But do you know 98% of the information on the Internet is in English? So what will English be like tomorrow?

(   )41. What is the passage mainly about?
　　A. Internet.　　B. Information.　　C. Computers.　　D. e-mails.

(   )42. Which is the quickest and cheapest way to send messages to your friends?

Unit 7　The Internet

　　　　A. By post.　　B. By e-mail.　　C. By telephone.　　D. By satellite.

(　　)43. Which may be the most possible place for people to work in tomorrow?

　　　　A. In the office.　B. At school.　　C. At home.　　D. In the company.

(　　)44. Who is the owner of the Internet?

　　　　A. The headmaster.　　　　　　B. The officer.

　　　　C. The user.　　　　　　　　　D. No one.

(　　)45. What does the writer try to tell us with the last two sentences?

　　　　A. English is important in using the Internet.

　　　　B. The Internet is more and more popular.

　　　　C. Most of the information is in English.

　　　　D. Every computer must have the Internet.

B

A teacher was asking a student a lot of questions but the student couldn't answer any of them. The teacher then decided to ask him very easy questions so that he could get a few rights. "Who was Beethoven(贝多芬)?" she asked.

The student thought for some time and then answered,"A king."

"No,he was a musician," the teacher said. She was getting a little angry now, but he was trying not to show it.

Then she asked,"Who was the first president of the USA?"

The student thought for a long time, but he didn't say anything. Then the teacher got very angry and shouted:"George Washington!" The student got up and begin to walk towards the door.

"Come back!" the teacher said. "I didn't tell you to go." "Oh, I'm sorry." the student said, "I thought you called the next student."

(　　)46. How many questions did the teacher ask the student?

　　　　A. One.　　B. Two.　　C. Three.　　D. Not mention it.

(　　)47. In this passage, the teacher asked this student very easy questions because she wanted him _____.

　　　　A. to get a few rights　　　　B. to answer difficult questions

　　　　C. to come back　　　　　　D. to go out

(　　)48. The student thought Beethoven was _____, but in fact Beethoven was _____.

　　　　A. a musician; a king　　　　B. a king; a teacher

　　　　C. a king; a musician　　　　D. a musician; a teacher

(　　)49. Who was George Washington?

— 123 —

A. A musician. B. The teacher's name.
C. A king. D. The first president of the USA.

( )50. From the passage, we can infer(推断) that _____.
A. this student is a good student
B. this student's study is not good
C. the teacher wanted to call the next student
D. the teacher asked the student to go

C

We are all busy talking about and using the Internet. But how many of us know the history of the Internet?

Many people are surprised when they find that the Internet was set up in the 1960's. At that time, computers were large and expensive. Computer networks didn't work well. If one computer in the network broke down, then the whole network stopped. So a new network system had to be set up. It should be good enough to be used many different computers. If part of the network was not working, information could be sent through another part. In this way computer network system would keep on working all the time.

At first the Internet was only used by the government. But in the early 1970's, universities, hospitals and banks are allowed to use it, too. However, computers were still very expensive and the Internet was difficult to use. By the start of the 1990's, computers became cheaper and easier to use. Scientists had also developed software that made "surfing" the Internet more convenient. Today it is easy to get on-line and it is said millions of people use the Internet every day. Sending e-mail is more and more popular among students.

The Internet has now become one of the most important parts of people's life.

( )51. The Internet has a history of more than _____ year.
A. sixty B. ten C. fifty D. twenty

( )52. A new network system was set up _____.
A. to make computers cheaper
B. to make itself keep on working all the time
C. to break down the whole networks
D. to make computers large and expensive

( )53. At first the Internet was only used by _____.
A. the government B. universities
C. hospital and banks D. schools

(　　)54. _____ made "surfing" the Internet more convenient.

A. Computers　　B. Scientists　　C. Software　　D. Information

(　　)55. Which of the following is true?

A. In the 1960's, computer networks worked well.

B. In the early 1970's, the Internet was easy to use.

C. Sending e-mail is more and more popular among students.

D. Today it is still not easy to get on-line.

第二节　词义搭配:从(B)栏中选出(A)栏单词的正确解释。(共10分,每小题1分)

　　　　　(A)　　　　　　　　　(B)

(　　)56. favorite　　A. a person who is going past sb./sth. by chance

(　　)57. fresh　　B. recently produced or picked

(　　)58. popular　　C. to give all your attention to sth. and not think about anything else

(　　)59. spare　　D. to like best

(　　)60. typical　　E. to make sth. such as time or money available to sb. or for sth.

(　　)61. passer-by　　F. a small symbol on a computer or smartphone screen

(　　)62. concentrate　　G. to undo the lock of a door, window, etc., using a key

(　　)63. icon　　H. that is not fixed in one place and can be moved

(　　)64. mobile　　I. having the usual qualities or features of a particular type of person, thing or group

(　　)65. unlock　　J. liked or enjoyed by a large number of people

第三节　补全对话。根据对话内容,从对话后的选项中选出能填入空白处的最佳选项。(共10分,每小题2分)

A:Excuse me, I'm doing a survey about online activities. Could you spare a few minutes?

B:OK.　66　

A:Would you like to surf the Internet?

B:　67　.

A:What activities do you usually do online?

B:I like chatting with my friends, reading news and playing games.

A:　68　

B:About two hours.

A:Why do you like online activities?

B:　69　. Besides, I can share feelings and experiences with my friends.

A:OK. Thank you for your time.

B：__70__.

A. How much time do you spend online every day?
B. They're really interesting.
C. What would you like to ask?
D. You are welcome.
E. Yes, I'd like to.

第三部分　语言技能运用

第一节　单词拼写：根据下列句子及所给汉语注释，在横线上写出该单词的正确形式。（共5分，每小题1分）

71. This is a _____ （典型的） painting of his early work.

72. This song is _____ （受欢迎的） among the teenagers.

73. I became _____ （爱发脾气的） when I lost a game.

74. What's the _____ （人口） of Hebei Province?

75. I'm doing a _____ （调查） about online games.

第二节　词形变换：用括号内所给词的适当形式填空。（共5分，每小题1分）

76. It was a sudden _____ (decide).

77. The _____ (solve) the problem required many hours.

78. Money does not always bring _____ (happy).

79. We will have a _____ (discuss) in English tomorrow.

80. He spent three day in _____ (read) the book.

第三节　改错：从A、B、C、D四个画线部分处找出一处错误的选项，填入相应题号后的括号内，并在横线上写出正确答案。（共10分，每小题2分）

81. He <u>has</u> given <u>us</u> <u>many</u> useful <u>suggestion</u>.
　　　A　　　B　　C　　　　D

82. <u>Listen</u>! <u>What</u> <u>are</u> the girls <u>do</u> now?
　　A　　　　B　　C　　　　　D

83. He <u>has</u> to work <u>if</u> he wants <u>to live</u> <u>comfortable</u>.
　　　A　　　　B　　　　C　　　D

84. It is much <u>easy</u> to make <u>plans</u> <u>than</u> to <u>carry them out</u>.
　　　　　　A　　　　　B　　　C　　　　D

85. He <u>was</u> <u>used</u> <u>to go</u> to <u>school</u> by <u>bike</u>.
　　　A　　B　　　　　C　　　　D

第四节　书面表达。（共10分）

作文题目：How to Use the Cellphone

词数要求:80~100 词

写作要点:1. 手机有很多用处:上网购物、玩游戏、聊天,搜索对学习有用的资料和信息等;
　　　　2. 沉溺于玩手机会影响学习,浪费时间。

Unit 8

People and Events

Warming up

一、句型汇结

1. What's your favorite…? 你最喜欢的是……?

2. Why do you like it most? 你为什么最喜欢它?

3. There are so many inventions, and they have changed our lives so much. 有这么多的发明,它们极大地改变了我们的生活。

4. I can't live without it. 没有它我活不下去。

5. I hope someday I can invent something useful. 希望有一天我也能发明件有用的东西。

6. It is well known in China because it was the first of its kind designed and built by Chinese people. 它在中国很有名,因为它是第一条由中国人设计并建造的铁路。

7. Born in 1861 in Guangdong Province, he showed an interest in machines at an early age. 他1861年出生于广东省,从小就对机械感兴趣。

8. Upon his graduation from Yale University in 1881, Zhan returned to China and began his work on the Jingzhang Railway in 1905. 1881年从耶鲁大学毕业后,詹天佑便回国并于1905年开始主持京张铁路的工作。

9. Zhan Tianyou overcame all kinds of difficulties and succeeded in finishing the task. 詹天佑克服了重重困难,成功完成了任务。

10. It is considered a brilliant piece of work in Chinese railway history. 它被认为是中国铁路史上的一项杰出工程。

二、英汉互译

1. 相信(v.)_____

2. 发明(v.)_____(n.)_____发明者(n.)_____

3. 杰出的（adj.）_____

4. 毕业(n.)_____(v.)_____毕业生(n.)_____

5. 设计(v.)_____(n.)_____设计者(n.)_____

6. schedule(n.)_____　　　　7. stretch(v.)_____

8. consider(v.)_____　　　　9. chief(adj.)_____

10. complete(v.)_____　　　11. ahead of schedule_____

12. ebook reader_____　　　13. return to_____

14. show an interest in_____　15. succeed in_____

Listening and Speaking

一、找出与所给单词画线部分读音相同的选项

(   ) 1. bel<u>ie</u>ve　　A. s<u>e</u>lfie　　B. ch<u>ie</u>f　　C. d<u>ie</u>　　D. l<u>ie</u>

(   ) 2. compl<u>e</u>te　A. m<u>e</u>ter　　B. <u>e</u>nough　C. b<u>e</u>cause　D. tick<u>e</u>t

(   ) 3. rec<u>o</u>rd　　A. c<u>o</u>lor　　B. d<u>o</u>ctor　　C. <u>o</u>rder　　D. inf<u>o</u>rmation

(   ) 4. ah<u>ea</u>d　　A. br<u>ea</u>k　　B. gr<u>ea</u>t　　C. id<u>ea</u>　　D. r<u>ea</u>dy

(   ) 5. sh<u>ow</u>　　　A. wind<u>ow</u>　B. d<u>ow</u>n　　C. br<u>ow</u>n　　D. h<u>ow</u>

二、从B栏中找出与A栏相对应的答语

A	B
1. What do you do?	A. I can do a lot of things with it.
2. What's your favorite invention?	B. About 2,000 years.
3. Why do you like it most?	C. The smartphone, of course.
4. Is it also your favorite invention?	D. I am a nurse.
5. How long is the history of using paper in China?	E. I'm afraid not.

三、用所给句子补全下面对话

A：What is your favorite invention?

B： 1 .

A：Why do you like it most?

B： 2 . Is it also your favorite invention?

A： 3 . I like the compass best.

B：Really? Why?

A：Well, 4 .

B：I see. There are so many inventions, and they have changed our lives so much.

A：That's true. I hope someday I can invent something useful.

B：Yeah. 5 .

> A. That would be cool
> B. because it's difficult to find directions without it
> C. I'm afraid not
> D. It has sped up the development of the world so much
> E. The computer, of course

四、场景模拟(主题对话)

假设你是一名教师,谈谈你认为对该职业较为重要的人或事。

_____

_____

_____

_____

_____

Reading and Writing

一、用括号内所给汉语提示或单词的适当形式填空

1. He is _____ (interest) in playing basketball.

Unit 8 People and Events

2. They succeeded in _____ (finish) the task.

3. It is well _____ (know) that Taiwan belongs to China.

4. He ought to stop _____ (smoke) right now.

5. After _____ (graduate), he became a teacher.

6. The building was _____ (design) by him.

7. The Smiths _____ (return) to China last year.

8. With the _____ (invent) of the train, people can travel long distances at a higher speed more easily.

9. The people are remembered for their _____ (contribute) to the great breakthrough.

10. China high-speed trains have become faster and _____ (fast).

二、完形填空

Who invented music? Who sang the first song? No one __1__ exactly(准确地) the answers to these questions. But we know that music is very __2__ in everyone's life.

Babies and young children would like someone __3__ to them. When they get older, they like to __4__ songs themselves. When children go to __5__, their world of music grows wide. In middle school, students __6__ music lessons. And they become __7__ in pop music. It will make __8__ happy.

We can __9__ hear music in other places such as shops and bars and so on. That's because that music can help people relax after __10__ hard work.

We couldn't imagine that without music what our life would be like.

(   )1. A. makes   B. knows   C. keeps   D. leaves

(   )2. A. enough   B. important   C. classical   D. simple

(   )3. A. sings   B. singing   C. to sing   D. sang

(   )4. A. talk   B. sing   C. listen   D. dance

(   )5. A. bed   B. shop   C. school   D. picnic

(   )6. A. make   B. teach   C. take   D. hate

(   )7. A. interested   B. interesting C. happy   D. careful

(   )8. A. us   B. you   C. them   D. him

(   )9. A. too   B. also   C. either   D. never

(   )10. A. a day   B. days   C. one-day's   D. a day's

三、阅读理解

Getting plenty of exercise is very important. I enjoy swimming very much. Last summer, I went to the beach every day. I plan to go there this summer too, but I may not be able to. I have a new job. Sometimes I have to work until late at night. Although I now work more hours than I used to, I do receive larger salary.

　　I didn't receive much pay on my old job. I like my new job, but I had known that if it would take up so much of my free time, I wouldn't have taken it. I prefer swimming to spending money.

　　I have heard that riding a bike is good exercise. Maybe I will be able to save enough money to buy a bike. My neighbor, Mrs. Wilson has a bike that I could borrow from her, but I would rather own my own bike. If I used hers, I would worry about damaging it. Since I make more money now, I think that I can afford to buy my own. Getting a bike is really a good idea, because while I am riding to and from work, I will be getting exercise at the same time. It's easier to get to the beach by bike, too. I might be able to go swimming every day after all. This new job is great! I'm very excited. This will be a summer full of exercise.

(　　) 1. Last summer, I went to the beach for _____.

　　　　A. riding　　　　B. swimming　　　　C. working　　　　D. walking

(　　) 2. The salary of my old job is _____.

　　　　A. as much as the new one　　　　B. a little more than the new one

　　　　C. more than the new one　　　　　D. less than the new one

(　　) 3. The working time of my new job is _____.

　　　　A. longer than the old one　　　　B. as long as the old one

　　　　C. shorter than the old one　　　　D. at night

(　　) 4. I like my new job because _____.

　　　　A. it would take up so much of my free time

　　　　B. it wouldn't take up so much of my free time

　　　　C. I will be able to save enough money to buy a bike

　　　　D. I could borrow a bike from my neighbor, Mrs. Wilson

(　　) 5. Which statement is NOT true according to the passage?

　　　　A. I might be able to ride my bike to go to the beach.

　　　　B. I could be getting exercise while I am riding to and from work.

　　　　C. I could ride my bike to go swimming.

　　　　D. I could make more money by riding my bike.

四、书面表达

写作题目:The Opinion of Using WeChat

词数要求:80~100 词

Unit 8　People and Events

写作要点:1. 微信给我们的生活带来的便利;
　　　　2. 微信使用过程中可能引发的问题。

_____

_____

_____

_____

_____

_____

Grammar

一、从下面每小题四个选项中选出最佳选项

(　　)1. —Could I use your dictionary?
　　　—Yes, of course you _____.
　　　A. could　　B. will　　C. can　　D. might

(　　)2. —_____ I take the magazine away?
　　　—No, you mustn't. You _____ read it only here.
　　　A. Must; can　　B. May; can　　C. Need; must　　D. Must; must

(　　)3. —Must I take a bus?
　　　—No, you _____. You can walk there.
　　　A. must not　　B. don't　　C. don't have to　　D. had better not to

(　　)4. —Are you going to Mike's party?
　　　—I'm not sure. I _____ go to the cinema instead.
　　　A. must　　B. would　　C. should　　D. might

(　　)5. One _____ punished for what he has not done.
　　　A. ought not to　　B. ought not to be　　C. ought to not　　D. ought not be

(　　)6. A computer _____ think for itself; it must be told what to do.
　　　A. can't　　B. mustn't　　C. may not　　D. might not

(　　)7. Excuse me, _____ you please pass me that cup?
　　　A. do　　B. should　　C. would　　D. must

(　　)8. —Are you in a hurry?

—No, in fact I've got plenty of time. I _____ wait.

A. must B. need C. may D. should

( ) 9. Her arm is all right. She _____ go and see the doctor.

A. has not to B. don't have to

C. haven't to D. doesn't have to

( ) 10. You _____ be late for school again next time.

A. mustn't B. needn't C. don't have to D. don't need to

( ) 11. —Must I do my homework at once?

—No, you _____.

A. needn't B. mustn't C. can't D. may not

( ) 12. You _____ worry about your daughter. She will get well soon.

A. needn't B. don't need C. needn't to D. doesn't need

( ) 13. —Is Peter coming by bus?

—He should, but he _____ not. He likes driving his car.

A. must B. can C. need D. may

( ) 14. You _____ out last night. I called you several times, but nobody answered.

A. must have been B. must be

C. might have been D. might be

( ) 15. Jeff _____ come to see us tonight, but he isn't very sure yet.

A. may B. can C. has to D. must

( ) 16. —He _____ be in the classroom, I think.

—No, he _____ be in the classroom. I saw him go home a minute ago.

A. can; may not B. must; may not

C. may; can't D. may; mustn't

( ) 17. You _____ practise the drums while the baby is sleeping.

A. needn't B. mightn't C. mustn't D. won't

( ) 18. You _____ him the news; he knew it already.

A. needn't tell B. needn't have told

C. mightn't tell D. mightn't have told

( ) 19. Are you still here? You _____ home hours ago.

A. should go B. should have gone

C. might go D. may have gone

( ) 20. I _____ have met him a long time ago. Both his name and face are very familiar.

Unit 8 People and Events

A. may   B. can   C. would   D. should

( )21. —Shall we go shopping?

—Sorry, we _____ buy anything now because none of the shops are open.

A. mustn't   B. needn't   C. can't   D. shouldn't

( )22. They often go to the restaurants for meals. They _____ be very poor.

A. mustn't   B. can't   C. may not   D. needn't

( )23. —Why didn't she come to the meeting yesterday?

—I'm so sure. She _____ ill.

A. should be   B. should have been

C. must be   D. might have been

( )24. —Is there a flight to London this evening?

—There _____ be. I'll phone the airport and find it out.

A. Must   B. might   C. would   D. can

( )25. A good friend is someone you _____ share your pleasure and pain with.

A. ought   B. need   C. can   D. must

( )26. —Mum, _____ I play football this afternoon?

—Sure, but you _____ finish your homework first.

A. may; could   B. can; must   C. can; mustn't   D. may; can't

( )27. —Must we finish the work today?

—_____. We have something else to do tomorrow.

A. Yes, we can   B. No, we can't

C. Yes, we must   D. No, we needn't

( )28. —Must I wait here all morning? I have a lot of work to do.

—No, you _____. You may be back in the afternoon.

A. mustn't   B. can't

C. don't have to   D. may not

( )29. —Shall we take a car?

—No, we _____. It's only five minutes' walk.

A. can't   B. mustn't   C. needn't   D. couldn't

( )30. The sweater _____ belong to Jim. It's much too large for him.

A. mustn't   B. can't   C. needn't   D. shouldn't

二、找出下列句子中错误的选项，并改正过来

1. You needn't to go shopping with me.
       A   B   C   D

2. I can help you last night, but you didn't come.
      A   B   C   D

3. He studied hard and could pass the exam.
        A   B   C   D

4. You have not to take a bus. You can walk there.
        A   B   C   D

5. From what I have seen and heard, I must say Chinese people are living happily.
     A   B   C   D

6. The house where he lives needs to repair at once.
            A   B   C   D

7. He may not be a doctor. He works in a bookstore.
      A B   C   D

8. It is too cold outside. You'd better to put on your coat.
      A B   C   D

9. Mrs. Brown must have seen the film last night, mustn't she?
           A   B   C   D

10. She used to getting up early when she was a child.
        A   B   C   D

For Better Performance

一、找出与所给单词画线部分读音相同的选项

(　　) 1. chat　　A. stomach　　B. chemistry　　C. chief　　D. chemical

(　　) 2. ahead　　A. bread　　B. cheap　　C. easy　　D. eat

(　　) 3. consider　　A. terminal　　B. order　　C. person　　D. term

(　　) 4. coffee　　A. need　　B. agree　　C. meet　　D. committee

(　　) 5. book　　A. flood　　B. choose　　C. cook　　D. moon

二、英汉互译

1. 聊天(v.)_____　　2. 克服(v.)_____
3. 记录(v.)_____　　4. 兴趣(n.)_____
5. believe(v.)_____　　6. invent(v.)_____
7. invention(n.)_____　　8. inventor(n.)_____
9. brilliant(adj.)_____　　10. graduation(n.)_____
11. graduate(v.&n.)_____　　12. design(v.)_____
13. designer(n.)_____　　14. chief(adj.)_____

三、用括号内所给汉语提示或单词的适当形式填空

1. You can tell that she is a _____ (foreign) from her face.
2. No, I _____ (agree). I don't think it is the right thing to do.
3. Throw away the pen. It is _____ (use).
4. A good _____ (begin) is half done.
5. You'd better not spend too much time in _____ (play) games.
6. What job are you _____ (interest) in?
7. Do you often make a _____ (decide) by yourself on important situation?
8. The _____ (hard) you study, the more progress you will make.
9. A good education is a good way to _____ (succeed) and independence.
10. With the _____ (develop) of 5G Technology, the use of mobile phone is getting more and more convenient.

四、找出下列句子中错误的选项，并改正过来

1. My watch must be ten minutes slowly.
     A   B   C   D
2. We don't need call him up; he will wake up of himself.
               A   B   C   D
3. People spent so much money in their pets.
          A B   C D
4. It is said that he used to spend five hours swim in the river.
     A   B   C   D
5. You'd better not to be late for the meeting again.
     A   B   C   D

单元检测

第一部分　英语知识运用

第一节　语音知识： 从 A、B、C、D 四个选项中找出其画线部分与所给单词画线部分读音相同的选项。（共 5 分，每小题 1 分）

(　) 1. design　　A. go　　　　B. graduation　　C. sign　　　D. growth
(　) 2. chief　　　A. Christmas　B. school　　　　C. machine　 D. chair
(　) 3. with　　　A. there　　　B. think　　　　 C. thank　　 D. truth

( )4. s<u>ur</u>prise   A. t<u>ur</u>n   B. h<u>ur</u>t   C. ret<u>ur</u>n   D. s<u>ur</u>round

( )5. que<u>stion</u>   A. inven<u>tion</u>   B. sugge<u>stion</u>   C. sta<u>tion</u>   D. gradua<u>tion</u>

第二节 词汇与语法知识：从 A、B、C、D 四个选项中选出可以填入空白处的最佳选项。（共 25 分，每小题 1 分）

( )6. Our country is becoming _____.
   A. strong and strong   B. stronger and stronger
   C. more stronger and more stronger   D. more and more strong

( )7. —Do we have to finish this work today?
   —Yes, you _____.
   A. can   B. may   C. must   D. need

( )8. I hope someday I can invent _____.
   A. useful something   B. something useful
   C. useful anything   D. anything useful

( )9. There are _____ inventions, and they have changed our lives _____.
   A. so much; so much   B. so many; so many
   C. so much; so many   D. so many; so much

( )10. He is considering _____ his job.
   A. change   B. changing   C. to change   D. changed

( )11. —Must I have in the plan of the meeting today?
   —No, you _____.
   A. mustn't   B. don't   C. may not   D. needn't

( )12. Mr. King works in _____ university. He likes taking _____ umbrella with him.
   A. an; an   B. a; a   C. an; a   D. a; an

( )13. It is said _____ a space station will be built on the moon in years to come.
   A. this   B. that   C. what   D. which

( )14. It's time for sports. Let's _____ swimming, shall we?
   A. go   B. to go   C. goes   D. going

( )15. You _____ to the meeting this afternoon if you have something important to do.
   A. needn't to come   B. don't need come
   C. don't need coming   D. needn't come

( )16. He must be from America, _____?
   A. mustn't he   B. needn't he   C. isn't he   D. may not he

( )17. Put on more clothes. You _____ be feeling cold with only a shirt on.

A. need   B. should   C. have to   D. must

(　　)18. My bike is broken. It needs _____.

A. to repair   B. repairing   C. repaired   D. be repaired

(　　)19. _____ wonderful advice it is!

A. What a   B. How a   C. What   D. How

(　　)20. The speech is very _____, and we were _____ to tears.

A. moved; moved   B. moving; moving   C. moving; moved   D. moved; moving

(　　)21. The classroom _____ now.

A. being cleaned   B. is being cleaned

C. cleaned   D. cleans

(　　)22. The two _____ didn't know what happened in the street.

A. passers-by   B. passer-bys   C. passers-bys   D. passer-by

(　　)23. Don't eat _____. You are _____ fat now.

A. too much; much too   B. too many; much too

C. much too; too much   D. too many; too much

(　　)24. It _____ be Miss Gao. I saw her go home just now.

A. can't   B. mustn't   C. needn't   D. won't

(　　)25. You hair is too long. You'd better have it _____.

A. cutting   B. to cutting   C. to cut   D. cut

(　　)26. My sister is good _____ physics while I do well _____ English.

A. at; in   B. at; with   C. in; at   D. with; at

(　　)27. Did you spend _____ hour _____ your homework yesterday?

A. an; do   B. an; did   C. a; doing   D. an; doing

(　　)28. I would like _____ basketball after school.

A. play   B. to play   C. playing   D. to playing

(　　)29. —I expect everything will turn out as you wish.

—_____.

A. All right   B. The same to you

C. No, thanks   D. I'd like to

(　　)30. George _____ have gone too far. His coffee is still warm.

A. must   B. can't   C. needn't   D. might

第三节　完形填空：阅读下面的短文，从所给的 **A、B、C、D** 四个选项中选出正确的答案。(共 **10** 分，每小题 **1** 分)

Who designed (设计) the first helicopter (直升机)? Who __31__ of the most famous pictures in the world? Who knew more about the human body than most __32__? There is an answer __33__ all. These questions—Leonardo de Vinci（达·芬奇）.

Leonardo may have been the greatest genius（天才）__34__ have ever known. He lived in Italy around the year 1500, but many of his inventions seem modern to us today. For example, one of his notebooks has drawings of a helicopter. Of course, he couldn't __35__ a helicopter with the things he had. But scientists say his idea would have worked. But Leonardo __36__ an inventor. He was one of the greatest artists of his day. By the time he was twenty years old, he was called a master（大师）painter, and as he got older he became __37__ more famous. Sometimes he drew a hand ten different ways __38__ he was ready to paint.

Many of Leonardo's wonderful paintings are still with __39__ today. You may know one of his most famous works the __40__ woman known as the Mona Lisa.

( )31. A. took   B. made   C. painted   D. invented
( )32. A. artists   B. doctors   C painters   D. people
( )33. A. to   B. of   C. for   D. from
( )34. A. the scientists B. the artists   C. the world   D. people
( )35. A. draw   B. paint   C. work   D. build
( )36. A. was just   B. wasn't just   C. wasn't   D. was no longer
( )37. A. less   B. no   C. even   D. very
( )38. A. before   B. after   C. because   D. when
( )39. A. him   B. us   C. them   D. you
( )40. A. interesting   B. crying   C. smiling   D. surprising

第二部分　篇章与词汇理解

第一节　阅读理解：阅读下面的短文，从每题所给的 A、B、C、D 四个选项中选出最恰当的答案。（共30分，每小题2分）

A

The designer of the Apple Computer, Steve Jobs, was not quite successful in his early years. He was not among the best students at school, and from time to time he got into trouble with either his schoolmates or his teachers. But he was full of new ideas, which few people saw the value of. Things remained the same when he went to college and he dropped out halfway.

Steve Jobs worked first as a video game designer at Atari. He worked there for only a few months and then he set out to India. He hoped that the trip would give him more ideas and give him a change in life for the better.

After he returned from India, he began to live on a farm in California. And then, in 1975,

Unit 8　People and Events

Steve Jobs set about making a new type of computer. Along with his friend Stephen Wozniak, he designed the Apple Computer in his bedroom and built it in his garage. He gave the name "Apple" because it reminded him of a happy summer he once had on an orchard(果园) in Oregon.

His Apple Computer was so successful that Steve Jobs soon became worldwide famous. But unluckily, he died of illness in 2011.

(　　)41. Steve Jobs _____ when he was in school.

　　A. was an outstanding student　　B. didn't do very well

　　C. was always praised by others　　D. didn't learn anything

(　　)42. The underlined word "value" in the first paragraph means _____.

　　A. beauty　　B. chance　　C. importance　　D. hope

(　　)43. Steve Jobs _____.

　　A. received an excellent college education

　　B. didn't go to college at all

　　C. studied in college for four years

　　D. didn't finish his college education

(　　)44. Steve Jobs named his computer company "Apple" because _____.

　　A. apple was his favorite fruit

　　B. he designed the computer under an apple tree

　　C. he wanted to remember the happy time on the orchard

　　D. the computer was designed on the orchard

(　　)45. Steve Jobs' _____ would be the most important thing for his lifetime success.

　　A. "failure" in school　　B. stay on the orchard

　　C. travel in India　　D. new ideas

B

Audio digital books(有声数字化图书) are becoming more and more popular these years. One of the reasons for this is that audio digital books can be "read" in many places comfortably.

The first favorite place of many people is in bed, before going to sleep. Many people like to lie in bed in the dark before they fall asleep at night. This would be the perfect time to listen to an audio digital book. If you read an ordinary book, the lights have to be turned on and you have to turn the pages with your hand. An audio digital book can just be listened to while a person stays comfortably in bed.

The next favorite place for many people listen to audio digital books would be in the kitchen. For some people kitchen chores are boring. Audio digital books provide good entertainment, and people don't need to turn pages.

An audio digital book is a favorite while a person is gardening. They can help take a person's mind off job at hand. It can be fun and exciting to do gardening with the help of these books.

An audio digital book is a favorite while a person is exercising. It allows the mind to be free while the legs, body and arms are kept busy. This would be a great place to listen to these books.

(　　)46. Why are audio digital books becoming more and more popular these years?

　　A. Because they are good.　　B. Because they are useful.

　　C. Because they are convenient.　　D. Because they are newest.

(　　)47. The second paragraph mainly tells us that _____.

　　A. the first favorite place for people to listen to audio digital books is in bed

　　B. one should lie in bed in the dark before falling asleep

　　C. an ordinary book cannot be listened to

　　D. you have to keep the lights on while reading ordinary books

(　　)48. Why do people like "reading" audio digital books in the kitchen?

　　A. Because they like reading books while cooking.

　　B. Because kitchen chores are boring.

　　C. Because they like listening to music while doing housework.

　　D. Because they provide good entertainment and people needn't turn pages.

(　　)49. What is his favorite choice when a person is exercising according to the passage?

　　A. Singing.　　B. "Reading" audio digital books.

　　C. Listening to music.　　D. Reading newspaper.

(　　)50. What is the passage mainly about?

　　A. What an audio digital book is.

　　B. How many kinds of audio digital books there are.

　　C. Why audio digital books are so popular.

　　D. Where people like to "read" audio digital books.

C

Paper is one of the most important products ever invented by man. The invention of paper meant that more people could be educated because more books could be printed. Paper provided an important way to communicate with knowledge.

Paper was first made in China about 2,000 years ago. In Egypt and the West, paper was not very commonly used before the year 1400. Paper was not made in southern Europe until about the year 1100. After that, the forestry countries of Canada, Sweden, Norway, Finland, and the United States became the most important paper-making countries. Today Finland makes the best paper in the world. And it has the biggest paper industry in the world. When we think of paper, we think of newspapers, books, letters, envelopes, and writing paper. So paper plays an important role in our lives.

Paper is very good for keeping you warm. Houses are often insulated with paper. You perhaps have seen homeless men sleep on a large number of newspapers. They are insulating themselves from the cold. In Finland, in winter it is sometimes 40 degrees below zero. The farmers wear paper boots in the snow. <u>Nothing could be warmer.</u>

( ) 51. What did the invention of paper mean?
   A. It meant more people could be educated.
   B. It meant more books could be printed.
   C. It meant paper is one of the most important products.
   D. It meant paper was invented by man.

( ) 52. When was paper made in southern Europe?
   A. Before 1100.　　B. After 1400.　　C. After 1100.　　D. Before 1400.

( ) 53. Which country makes the best paper?
   A. Norway.　　　　　　　　　　B. Canada.
   C. The United States.　　　　　　D. Finland.

( ) 54. What's the meaning of the underlined sentence "Nothing could be warmer"?
   A. Books are warmer.　　　　　　B. Newspapers are warmer.
   C. Paper is the warmest.　　　　　D. Houses are the warmest.

( ) 55. What's the main idea of the passage?
   A. The invention of paper.　　　　B. The best paper.
   C. The paper-making.　　　　　　D. The uses of paper.

第二节　词义搭配:从(B)栏中选出(A)栏单词的正确解释。(共10分,每小题1分)

　　　　(A)　　　　　　　　　　(B)

( ) 56. graduate　　　　A. to make sth. longer, wider or looser

( ) 57. invent　　　　　B. to feel certain that sth. is true

( ) 58. stretch　　　　　C. to talk to sb. in a friendly way

( ) 59. believe　　　　　D. to complete a course in education

( ) 60. chat　　　　　　E. to make up, think of, or produce for the first time

( ) 61. schedule　　　　F. to succeed in dealing with or controlling a problem

( ) 62. complete　　　　G. to think about sth. carefully

( ) 63. overcome　　　　H. most important

( ) 64. consider　　　　I. to finish making or doing sth.

( ) 65. chief　　　　　　J. a plan that lists all the work that you have to do

第三节 补全对话。根据对话内容，从对话后的选项中选出能填入空白处的最佳选项。（共10分，每小题2分）

A：Hey, Wang Hua. I saw there's a paper-making museum nearby. Should I go there?

B： 66 . Paper-making is an important part of Chinese culture and history.

A：I didn't know that! Could you teach me a little bit about it?

B：Sure. 67 .

A：That's a long time.

B：It is. And in the Han Dynasty, a man named Cai Lun greatly improved the method of paper-making.

A：How did he improve it? I mean, 68 ?

B：Because the quality was better, and the price was lower.

A： 69 . So, more people could buy paper and use it to record and share knowledge.

B：You're right. And Cai Lun's method of paper-making was later learned by people in other parts of the world.

A： 70 .

> A. why was his paper better
> B. Yeah, it's a good idea
> C. The history of using paper in China is about 2,000 years long.
> D. Cool
> E. I see

第三部分　语言技能运用

第一节　单词拼写：根据下列句子及所给汉语注释，在横线上写出该单词的正确形式。（共5分，每小题1分）

71. I can do a lot of things with the _____（智能手机）.

72. There are many _____（发明）in the world.

73. The _____（总的）engineer for this railway was Zhan Tianyou.

74. They have overcome many _____（困难）.

75. Jeff showed an _____（兴趣）in math when he was quite young.

第二节　词形变换：用括号内所给词的适当形式填空。（共5分，每小题1分）

76. He was _____ (interest) in drawing at an early age.

77. Mary likes _____ (chat) with her friends online.

78. Finally he gave up _____ (smoke).

79. Their names should be _____ (remember).

80. Great inventions help people live a better and _____ (happy) life.

第三节 改错:从 A、B、C、D 四个画线部分处找出一处错误的选项填入相应题号后的括号内,并在横线上写出正确答案。(共 10 分,每小题 2 分)

81. Much money spent on books every year.
     A   B   C   D

82. They managed getting the work done with very little help.
                  A   B   C   D

83. Mother asks me don't to play computer games before finishing my Homework.
                   A   B   C   D

84. The windows of the house need to paint.
         A   B   C   D

85. He was used to go to school by bike.
        A   B   C   D

第四节 书面表达。(共 10 分)

写作题目:Mobile Payment

词数要求:80~100 词

写作要点:1. 手机支付变得越来越流行;
        2. 你对手机支付的看法。

参考答案

Unit 1 Personal and Family Life

Warming up

1. 社区   2. 精力充沛的   3. 尤其   4. 介绍   5. 经理   6. 职业的

7. gift   8. puppy   9. talk about   10. festival   11. family name

Listening and Speaking

一、1-5　BACBB

二、1-5　BADEC

三、1-5　CABDE

四、场景模拟

A：Hello, mom. This is my friend, Mary. She comes from Shanghai. She works as a maths teacher in a middle school.

B：Hi! Mary. Nice to meet you!

C：Nice to meet you, too. It's an honor to know a beautiful lady like you.

B：Thank you.

…

Reading and Writing

一、1. community   2. energetic   3. especially   4. handmade   5. jogging

　　6. manages   7. parents   8. strict   9. preparing   10. named

二、1-5 CBBBC 6-10 ACDDC

三、1-5 DCCBB

四、书面表达

My best friend

I have many friends. I want to introduce my best friend to you. Cherry is my best friend from Handan, and she is a girl. She is very smart and beautiful. She likes singing dancing and shopping. She is good at maths, English and Chinese. She often helps me do my homework, so I make a great progress in my lessons now. Of course she also likes playing ping-pong, and her ping-pong skill is great, and always enjoy themselves with her ping-pong friends. Do you want to know more information about Cherry? Oh, I would like to introduce more information about her to you next time.

Grammar

一、1-5 CCDCA 6-10 AACDB 11-15 BAACA 16-20 BBADC 21-25 ABAAB

26-30 ABDCB

二、1. B 改为 doing 2. C 改为 becomes 3. B 改为 travels

4. D 改为 has 5. B 改为 want 6. B 改为 do 7. B 改为 does

8. B 改为 come 9. D 改为 has he 10. B 改为去掉

For Better Performance

一、1-5 ABDDC

二、1. be strict with 2. high school 3. younger sister

4. vocational school 5. especially 6. 手工制作的

7. 担任 8. 快递员 9. 照顾、照料 10. 注意

三、1. delivery 2. holding 3. especially 4. energetic 5. lives

6. introduce 7. handmade 8. younger 9. educating 10. jogging

四、1. C 改为 full 2. B 改为 yourselves 3. D 改为 ours 4. D 改为 with 5. C 改为 what

单元检测

第一部分

第一节　1-5 ACAAD

第二节　6-10 CCCBC　11-15 BABAD　16-20 DCCAB　21-25 CADDA
　　　　26-30 BACCA

第三节　31-35 BADCB　36-40 CADAC

第二部分

第一节　41-45 DCBCD　46-50 DABCC　51-55 BDBAB

第二节　56-60 EBACD　61-65 GFJHI

第三节　66-70 CEADB

第三部分

第一节　71. vocational　72. visited　73. cooking　74. especially　75. festivals

第二节　76. preparing　77. speaking　78. visiting　79. traveling　80. interested

第三节　81. B 改为 ask　82. D 改为 to do　83. B 改为 do　84. B 改为 does
　　　　85. D 改为 doesn't

第四节　书面表达

My Family

I have a happy family. My family have five people: grandpa, grandma, father, mother, and me. My parents and me live in city. My father is a worker. His work is hard. My mother works as a Chinese teacher in a vocational school. In the afternoon she doesn't go home. In the evening, she makes supper. The food is delicious. I am a student. I have Chinese, math and English everyday. My grandparents are farmers, and they live in a small village.

This is my happy family. My family is full of love and warmth. I love my family.

Unit 2　Transportation

Warming up

1. 地址　2. 方向　3. 租用　4. 省　5. 公交车站　6. visitor

7. convenient   8. airport   9. get off   10. rush hour

Listening and Speaking

一、1-5 CBADC

二、1-5 EACBD

三、1-5 CDAEB

四、场景模拟

A: Good morning, I'm Lihua, an exchange student here.

B: Good morning! I'm Li Yang from IT class, grade 1.

A: Excuse me, could you tell me how to get to the library?

B: Of course. Keep going in this direction and turn left at Teaching Building 1. Then go along the road and turn right. Turn left again at the first crossing. Then you will see the library on your left.

A: Keep going and turn left at...you lost me there.

B: Why don't we go there together?

A: Really? That's very kind of you!

Reading and Writing

一、1. address   2. airport   3. convenient   4. direction   5. district
    6. province   7. subway   8. taxi   9. visitor   10. changeable

二、1-5 BADCC   6-10 ACABB

三、1-5 CBCAC

四、书面表达

The Ways of Transportation

There are many ways of transportation currently, such as taxi, bus and bicycle. However, every kind of transportation has its own pros and cons.

For instance, travelling by bicycle is a good type of exercise. It helps us to maintain a healthy body. But it will take us a long time to get to a place far away. Taxi is a better option because it is convenient and relatively affordable. However, it is difficult to get a taxi during the rush hour.

Bus is very convenient, cheap and punctual. But sometimes there is no bus service going to the place we want to get to.

Therefore, I think we should choose the type of transportation wisely depending on our destinations.

Grammar

一、1-5 BCACB   6-10 ACBCB   11-15 ADCBA   16-20 CCAAB   21-25 AAAAC

  26-30 BCCAC

二、1. A 改为 Don't   2. A 改为 Work   3. B 改为 don't be   4. D 改为 will you

  5. D 改为 will you   6. C 改为 or   7. A 改为 bring   8. A 改为 Walk

  9. B 改为 read   10. B 改为 don't

For Better Performance

一、1-5 DCBAD

二、1. 换乘   2. 区   3. 快线   4. 地铁   5. 航站楼   6. shuttle bus

  7. worry about   8. had better   9. get to   10. take a taxi

三、1. visitors   2. express   3. terminal   4. Change   5. hired

  6. green   7. entrance   8. turning   9. careful   10. comfortable

四、1. D 改为 by   2. B 改为 drive   3. B 改为 in   4. A 改为 It   5. C 改为 half an hour

单元检测

第一部分

第一节 1-5 CDACA

第二节 6-10 AADDC   11-15 BCADB   16-20 ACDAA   21-25 AABDA

    26-30 DACBA

第三节 31-35 ADCBC   36-40 BBCAA

第二部分

第一节 41-45 BCDAB   46-50 DACCD   51-55 ADCAC

第二节 56-60 IEADG   61-65 JHFBC

第三节 66-70 CEABD

第三部分

第一节 71. near 72. exit 73. passenger 74. crossroads 75. expensive

第二节 76. worried 77. greener 78. careful 79. northern 80. different

第三节 81. B 改为 get to 82. A 改为 By the way 83. C 改为 about

84. A 改为 It 85. C 改为 on

第四节 书面表达

The Way of Going to School

Nowadays, students can go to school by bus, by bike, on foot or in their parents' cars.

Taking a bus is a good way. It is fast and cost less. But it produces gases that pollute the air. A car is fast way, too. But we have to spend a lot of money to buy it. Besides, too many cars on the road would cause traffic jams and it also produces bad gases. Riding to school is a good way. It causes no pollution, but it is slower than a bus or a car. Going on foot is the cheapest way of the all. It needs nothing but our own feet. It is the most environmentally friendly way. But it also the slowest way.

Unit 3 Shopping

Warming up

1. 交流 2. 和……比较 3. 适合 4. offer…to 5. lead the way to 6. on sale

7. 用……支付 8. shop assistant 9. payment code 10. 物质资料 11. traditional

12. original

Listening and Speaking

一、1-5 CABCB

二、1-5 EDACB

三、1-5 CDBEA

四、场景模拟

S-shop assistant   M-mother   J- Jane

— 6 —

S:What can I do for you?

M:I'd like to buy a dress for my daughter. Do you have some in new styles?

S:Yes, what about this red ones?

M:Do you like these ones, dear Jane?

J:Oh, no, I don't like the color, do you have some light green ones?

S:Yes, they are over there. I'll get one for you.

J:Can I try it on?

S:Of course, the fitting room is over there.

M:Oh, dear. It fits you well.

J:Yes, I'll take it.

M:How much is it?

S:It's 100 yuan. How will you pay for it?

M:Is credit card available?

S:Sorry, the machine can't work today.

M:Can I pay with my cellphone?

S:Yes, please show me your payment code … OK, Here is the dress. Thank you for shopping here.

Reading and Writing

一、1. communicate 2. tightly 3. traditional 4. made 5. fitting

6. Compared 7. discount 8. styles 9. offer 10. material

二、1-5 BDBCD 6-10 BADCA

三、1-5 DDCBB

四、书面表达

The Supermarket Nearby

The Huiyou supermarket is well known in our city. You have probably been there. It is situated near the public library. We usually call it a "one-stop market". This market contains a wide variety of goods. We are able to do most of our shopping in it at the same time. Additionally, it is a nice place for the house women to kill some time in the evening or on weekends. They can spend hours wandering around it and buy something for their family.

Grammar

一、1-5 ABCAB　6-10 CACCA　11-15 AAADB　16-20 CDDCD　21-25 ABDAB
　　26-30 BCBCA

二、1. D 改为 has　2. C 改为 before　3. A 改为 How　4. B 改为 to teach
　　5. D 改为 don't you　6. A 改为 Compared　7. B 改为 going to　8. D 改为 with
　　9. D 改为 a larger size　10. C 改为 better

For Better Performance

一、1-5 AADDC

二、1. save time　2. at any time　3. lower price
　　4. There are more products for you to choose
　　5. more information about the product　6. 用英语　7. 两者都
　　8. 和……比　9. 传统中国文化　10. 像……一样

三、1. history　2. discount　3. information　4. inconvenience　5. traditional
　　6. inconvenient　7. easier　8. creations　9. interested　10. tall

四、1. C 改为 to　2. A 改为 much　3. B 改为 sitting　4. B 改为 not to
　　5. D 改为 asking　6. B 改为 of　7. A 改为 whose　8. B 改为 does
　　9. C 改为 well　10. C 改为 are

单元检测

第一部分

第一节　1-5 BACCB

第二节　6-10 DAAAC　11-15 AAABA　16-20 CABAD　21-25 CBCCB
　　　　26-30 AABCB

第三节　31-35 DBDAD　36-40 ACBBD

第二部分

第一节　41-45 BADAB　46-50 DCCBA　51-55 BCDDC

第二节　56-60 IDACB　61-65 EJFGH

第三节　66-70　EDCAB

第三部分

第一节　71. attention　72. accept　73. development　74. government　75. traditional

第二节　76. uncomfortable　77. unluckily　78. friendship　79. harmful　80. twentieth

第三节　81. D 改为 swimming　82. C 改为 is　83. C 改为 I can

84. D 改为 didn't he　85. C 改为 travel

第四节　书面表达

Shopping Online

We talked about the advantages and disadvantages of online shopping these days. Some students think it's very convenient for us to go shopping on the Internet. The shops on Internet, for example taobao.com, 360buy.com are open for almost 24 hours a day so we can buy something we want at any time if we like. What's more, we needn't wait in a queue.

However, some students disagreed with them. We can't see the things while we are shopping. So we are not sure whether they are good or not. Besides, we can't enjoy the happiness of shopping with our friends.

Unit 4　School Life

Warming up

1. 信息技术　2. 喜欢做　3. 很有趣　4. 有用而且有趣　5. 上课　6. 举行比赛

7. 从……到　8. have practical training class　9. basic subjects　10. prepare…for

11. choose…from　12. be related to

Listening and Speaking

一、1-5　DDAAC

二、1-5　CDEBA

三、1-5　BACED

四、场景模拟

A：Hi, Tom. How are you going these days?

B：Oh, couldn't be better.

A：How do you like your new school?

B：I like it very much.

A：What's your favorite subject?

B：My favorite subject is science and technology.

A：Why do you like it so much.

B：I like it because it has a lot of fun, and I think it is useful and interesting.

...

Reading and Writing

一、1. chemistry   2. competition   3. internship   4. skill   5. favorite
   6. singing   7. relaxing   8. relative   9. excited   10. experienced

二、1-5 ACDBA   6-10 DBAAD

三、1-5 DCCDD

四、书面表达

Surfing the Internet

More and more people like to surf the Internet now. Surfing the Internet is one of the most important activities today. We can get plenty of information from the Internet. Some people say the world is smaller than before because of Internet.

If you want to know the answers to some unknown questions, just turn on the computer and surf the Internet. However, as students, we should not spend too much time in surfing the Internet every day. There is also something bad on the Internet. Therefore, it is important for us to tell the good things from bad things when we surf the Internet.

Grammar

一、1-5 CDDDD   6-10 BCDBB   11-15 DCCCB   16-20 DBACB   21-25 BBCBA
   26-30 AADAD

二、1. D 改为 get married   2. A 改为 Will   3. D 改为 are completed

4. A 改为 am leaving   5. A 改为 will   6. A 改为 will   7. C 改为 going

8. C 改为 will give   9. D 改为 is going to snow   10. A 改为 Will

For Better Performance

一、1-5 CAAAA

二、1. 在公司实习   2. 参加学校旅行   3. 加入学校俱乐部   4. 完成一份工作报告

5. 准备讨论   6. practice skill at skill training center   7. the most important thing

8. be different from   9. a good way to learn skills   10. of course

11. decide to do   12 no more than

三、1. college   2. exciting   3. Practice   4. Politics   5. preparing

6. decision   7. interested   8. skilled   9. making   10. useful

四、1. C 改为 to   2. B 改为 is different from   3. B 改为 is   4. B 改为 playing basketball

5. B 改为 to

单元检测

第一部分

第一节   1-5 ABDCC

第二节   6-10 ACCAB   11-15 AAABA   16-20 BBCAC   21-25 CBCAB

26-30 DCCDD

第三节   31-35 ABDCA   36-40 ABBCD

第二部分

第一节   41-45 DBBAB   46-50 ACDDC   51-55 DCACD

第二节   56-60 JBFGE   61-65 CDIHA

第三节   66-70 FADCE

第三部分

第一节   71. attention   72. information   73. relax   74. favorite   75. history

第二节   76. beginning   77. interested   78. experienced   79. related   80. difference

第三节   81. B 改为 will leave   82. A 改为 be   83. A 改为 will be

84. C 改为 that   85. A 改为 On

第四节　书面表达

My School Life

　　My school life is very common. I get up at six o'clock every morning from Monday to Friday. And then I would go running with my classmates, as our head teacher says health is the most important thing. After running I have to do morning exercises on the playground. Then I can have breakfast. Having breakfast, I need to have morning reading. Oh, I almost forget that all of the students have to do some cleaning before breakfast. There come the various classes. Then noon comes. After lunch, I will go to sleep. I often read twenty minutes before I fall asleep. I have class in the afternoon. And I still have classes at night. It's boring, right? But I have got used to it and enjoy myself at school.

Unit 5　Celebrations

Warming up

1. 宴会　2. birthday party　3. 邀请　4. opening ceremony　5. 欢迎宴会

6. welcome party　7. 如何,怎样　8. want　9. 当然　10. great

Listening and Speaking

一、1-5 ACDBA

二、1-5 BDEAC

三、1-5 CADEB

四、场景模拟

A：Hi, Peter. We'll have a three-day holiday. What are you going to do?

B：Nothing special. What about you?

A：I'm going to my hometown with my parents.

B：For what?

A：To celebrate the Dragon Boat Festival.

B：What kind of festival is it?

A：It's a traditional festival in China. It's in memory of Qu Yuan and has a history of more than 2,000 years.

B：How will you celebrate it?

A：We'll eat zongzi and watch the dragon boat racing. Would you like to go with us? We can celebrate it together.

B：Great, I'd love to. Thanks a lot.

A：You're welcome!

Reading and Writing

一、1. support   2. opening   3. held   4. sincerely   5. partners

   6. opportunity   7. seeing   8. behalf   9. confirm   10. invitation

二、1-5 ACADB   6-10 ADCAB

三、1-5 ABDDC

四、书面表达

Dear Mr. Black,

On behalf of our class, I'm writing to invite you to come to our welcome party.

In order to welcomethe exchange student Peter, we'll hold a party at 7:00 p.m. next Friday. It will be held in the dining hall of our school. At the party, we're going to have many activities, such as singing, dancing and playing games. Then we will exchange gifts after the party. We hope you can make a welcome speech at the beginning of the party. I believe your arrival will make us very happy.

Please confirm whether you can join us by this Saturday. I'm looking forward to hearing from you.

Yours,

Li Hua

Grammar

一、1-5 BCDBB   6-10 ACBDA   11-15 CACBD   16-20 CDCBA   21-25 CABCA

   26-30 DCACD

二、1. for two years   2. has been away   3. has not   4. What has   5. has had/kept

   6. have; heard   7. How long   8. Has; finished   9. has she   10. has been on

英语 1 知识点强化练习

For Better Performance

一、1-5 BADCA

二、1. 出席,参加   2. beat   3. 庆祝   4. ceremony   5. 雇员   6. confirm
   7. 共同的   8. look forward to   9. 代表   10. play an important role

三、1. cafeteria   2. event   3. invite   4. marketing   5. attend
   6. banquet   7. common   8. role   9. employees   10. celebrated

四、1. B 改为 preparing   2. C 改为 been dead   3. A 改为 is   4. D 改为 success
   5. D 改为 to look forward to

单元检测

第一部分

第一节   1-5 ACBDB

第二节   6-10 ADBCD   11-15 ACBDA   16-20 BDABC   21-25 BADCB
       26-30 ACBCD

第三节   31-35 ACDBA   36-40 CDBCB

第二部分

第一节   41-45 ABCBD   46-50 ABCCD   51-55 CADCB

第二节   56-60 EHAJF   61-65 CIGDB

第三节   66-70 BADEC

第三部分

第一节   71. beat   72. ceremony   73. common   74. confirmed   75. preparations

第二节   76. attendance   77. celebrate   78. employee   79. growth   80. invitation

第三节   81. C 改为 has gone to   82. B 改为 invitation   83. C 改为 knows
       84. A 改为 held   85. C 改为 for

第四节   书面表达

Dear Mr. Smith,

On behalf of our class, I'm writing to invite you to come to our party to celebrate the Spring Festival.

Our traditional festival—the Spring Festival is coming. We're going to hold a party at 4:00

next Saturday afternoon in the music classroom of our school. We will sing, dance and eat dumplings. We are going to make a team to act Beijing opera and invite you to be one of the members. Please wear a white shirt and a pair of black trousers. We are going to take a photo together in the music classroom after the party.

Please confirm whether you can join us by this weekend. I'm looking forward to hearing from you.

Yours,

Li Ming

Unit 6 Food and Drinks

Warming up

1. 饺子   2. mineral water   3. 牛排   4. salad   5. 布丁   6. chicken

7. 橙汁   8. Mapo Tofu   9. 糖醋鱼   10. spicy   11. 咸的   12. sour

Listening and Speaking

一、1-5 ACBDB

二、1-5 DEACB

三、1-5 BDACE

四、场景模拟

A：What's the best restaurant in our city?

B：Noodle House.

A：What's the specialty of it?

B：All kinds of noodles.

A：Are they delicious?

B：Of course, the noodles there are very delicious.

A：Are they expensive?

B：Yes, it's kind of expensive. But the service is great.

A：OK, let's go and have a try.

B：All right.

Reading and Writing

一、1. order   2. medium   3. recommend   4. specialty   5. mineral

6. mushrooms   7. variety   8. factor   9. quality   10. cuisine

二、1-5 BADCA   6-10 BCBDA

三、1-5 BACCD

四、书面表达

Would you like to come to Good Luck Restaurant to have Chinese dishes?

Good Luck Restaurant is 200 meters away from the West Lake, across from a supermarket. You can walk here after visiting the West Lake. We have Dongpo Pork and Kung Pao Chicken, either of which is 25 yuan. There are also many kinds of delicious vegetables in our restaurant, and each of them is at most 15 yuan. We also provide noodles, rice and steamed bread. We also have various juice. The specialty in our restaurant is West Lake Vinegar Fish, which is only 40 yuan. I believe you can enjoy your meal in our restaurant.

Grammar

一、1-5 BCABD   6-10 CABDA   11-15 CDBCB   16-20 DCABC   21-25 ABCDB

26-30 DBACC

二、1. These；photos   2. How much progress   3. How many   4. dictionaries are

5. parents；teachers   6. notes are   7. owner；supermarket   8. subjects；English

9. sheep are   10. is；tomato

For Better Performance

一、1-5 BCDAB

二、1. 温暖舒适的   2. dinning   3. 因素   4. medium   5. 蘑菇   6. quality

7. 推荐   8. variety   9. 各种各样的   10. specialty   11. 合适的   12. restaurant

13. 菜肴   14. order

三、1. dinning   2. contribute   3. attention   4. rare   5. wisely

6. Spicy 7. proper 8. various 9. able 10. range

四、1. C 改为 fruit   2. A 改为 eating   3. B 改为 to go   4. B 改为 cuisines

5. C 改为 different

单元检测

第一部分

第一节　1-5 BCADB

第二节　6-10 ADCAC   11-15 BCDCA   16-20 CDCAB   21-25 CBADB

　　　　26-30 BDACC

第三节　31-35 CADBC   36-40 ABCBD

第二部分

第一节　41-45 ABBDC   46-50 CBACD   51-55 CBADC

第二节　56-60 BFJAH   61-65 CDGEI

第三节　66-70 CAEBD

第三部分

第一节　71. environment   72. famous   73. proper   74. recommend   75. restaurant

第二节　76. mushrooms   77. ordered   78. ruined   79. specialty   80. unwise

第三节　81. A 改为 choose   82. B 改为 much   83. B 改为 contributes

　　　　84. C 改为 different   85. C 改为 depending

第四节　书面表达

Dear Peter,

I hear that you plan to choose a restaurant to taste the local food this weekend. I think Friendship Restaurant is the best, which is close to our school. There are many kinds of delicious food in the restaurant, such as fried fish, dumplings with seafood and various noodles. And the specialty is roast duck, which attracts many customers every day. The restaurant is very large and the food is fresh. The most important thing is that the price is reasonable and the service is wonderful.

I believe you can enjoy yourself there.

Yours,

Li Hua

Unit 7　The Internet

Warming up

1. 点击　2. 想要的　3. 图标　4. 自拍照片　5. 外卖的　6. passer-by　7. popular

8. spare　9. typical　10. interview　11. concentrate on　12. go over

13. have access to　14. log onto　15. stay up

Listening and Speaking

一、1-5 DCDCC

二、1-5 EADCB

三、1-5 BAECD

四、场景模拟

A：Have you ever had classes online?

B：Sure. I have about 10 online classes every week.

A：Why did you like having classes online?

B：It is quite convenient. We can listen to our teacher, have discussions and do our homework in the online classroom.

…

Reading and Writing

一、1. convenient　2. typical　3. poems　4. take-out　5. favorite　6. fresh

　　7. share　8. experiences　9. information　10. comfortable

二、1-5 CDBAB　6-10 ABDCA

三、1-5 ACBDA

四、书面表达

Talking about Exploring the Internet

Generally speaking, the Internet is playing a more and more important part in our everyday life. Through the Internet we can read news both from home and abroad and get a lot of useful information as well. We can also send e-mails, take classes, read all kinds of books and learn foreign languages by ourselves, enjoy music, watch sports, play chess and so on. Besides, we can even do shopping, have a chat with others and make friends with them on the Internet.

But it also has many bad effects. For example, there are some unhealthy materials on web which will do harm to teenagers. And there are some games that can easily attract the students. So many students will waste a lot of valuable time.

On the whole, exploring the Internet will give us both good and bad things. We should make good use of the Internet. Only in this way can we benefit from it.

Grammar

一、1-5 BADAA   6-10 ACCDC   11-15 CACBC   16-20 DBCDB   21-25 CCBAB

　　26-30 BCCCC

二、1. C 改为 doing   2. B 改为 is   3. A 改为 are   4. C 改为 is singing   5. C 改为 playing

For Better Performance

一、1-5 CBADB

二、1. 新鲜的   2. 发出铃声   3. 可移动的   4. 诗   5. 调查   6. 过去常常

　　7. comfortable   8. necessary   9. population   10. smartphone

三、1. playing   2. playing   3. playing   4. carefully   5. desired

　　6. depending   7. suggestions   8. taller   9. singing   10. silent

四、1. C 改为 doing   2. B 改为 much   3. A 改为 is ringing

　　4. A 改为 depend on   5. A 改为 sending

单元检测

第一部分

第一节   1-5 DBDAC

第二节   6-10 DBACB   11-15 DCACB   16-20 CBAAD   21-25 DBCAB

　　　　26-30 CADDC

第三节   31-35 BBCAC   36-40 CADBB

第二部分

第一节 41-45 ABCDA 46-50 DACDB 51-55 ABACC

第二节 56-60 DBJEI 61-65 ACFHG

第三节 66-70 CEABD

第三部分

第一节 71. typical 72. popular 73. bad-tempered 74. population 75. survey

第二节 76. decision 77. solution 78. happiness 79. discussion 80. reading

第三节 81. D 改为 suggestions 82. D 改为 doing 83. D 改为 comfortably

84. A 改为 easier 85. A 改为去掉 was

第四节 书面表达

How to Use the Cellphone

My mother bought me a cellphone on my birthday last week. I found it so useful and interesting. Despite playing games, chatting with e-pals and watching movies, I could also use it to book tickets, buy something necessary, and search for studying materials. However, sometimes I got addicted to it so that I wasted a lot of time, so my mother took it away from me and warned me not to use again if I couldn't make good use of it. I promised (to my mother) to control myself and make it beneficial to me.

Unit 8 People and Events

Warming up

1. believe 2. invent; invention; inventor 3. brilliant 4. graduation; graduate; graduate
5. design; design; designer 6. 工作计划；日程安排 7. 延伸 8. 认为；考虑
9. 总的；主要的 10. 完成 11. 提前 12. 电子书阅读器 13. 返回
14. 对……感兴趣 15. 在……取得成功

Listening and Speaking

一、1-5 BACDA

二、1-5 DCAEB

三、1-5 EDCBA

四、场景模拟

A：What do you do?

B：I am a teacher.

A：Can you think of an important person or event related to your work?

B：The invention of the Internet.

A：Why?

B：Because I can give online classes to teach students in remote areas.

Reading and Writing

一、1. interested　2. finishing　3. known　4. smoking　5. graduation
　　6. designed　7. returned　8. invention　9. contribution　10. faster

二、1-5 BBCBC　6-10 CACBD

三、1-5 BDACD

四、书面表达

The Opinions of Using WeChat

As we all know, WeChat plays a more and more important role in our life. We use WeChat because it can provide a way for us to communicate with each other, and we can use some functions of WeChat to make new friends and we can also learn so many things.

But every coin has two sides, we should be careful because so many students spend too much time on it. They can't finish their homework on time. Sometimes they may meet e-pals without parents, but most of all, phones will make us shortsightedness.

On the whole, if we make full use of WeChat, we'll benefit a lot from it.

Grammar

一、1-5 CBCDB　6-10 ACCDA　11-15 AADAA　16-20 CCBBA　21-25 CBDBC
　　26-30 BCCCB

二、1. A 应改为 go　2. A 应改为 could　3. C 应改为 was able to

— 21 —

4. A 改为 don't have to 5. C 改为 can 6. D 改为 to be repaired/repairing

7. A 改为 can't 8. D 改为 put on 9. D 改为 didn't she 10. B 改为 get up

For Better Performance

一、1-5 CABDC

二、1. chat 2. overcome 3. record 4. interest 5. 相信 6. 发明 7. 发明 8. 发明者 9. 杰出的 10. 毕业 11. 毕业;毕业生 12. 设计 13. 设计师 14. 总的;主要的

三、1. foreigner 2. disagree 3. useless 4. beginning 5. playing 6. interested 7. decision 8. harder 9. success 10. development

四、1. D 改为 slow 2. A 改为 to call 3. C 改为 on 4. D 改为 swimming 5. B 改为 not be

单元检测

第一部分

第一节 1-5 CDADB

第二节 6-10 BCBDB 11-15 DDBAD 16-20 CDBCC 21-25 BAAAD
         26-30 ADBBB

第三节 31-35 CBADD 36-40 BCABC

第二部分

第一节 41-45 BCDCD 46-50 CADBC 51-55 ACDCD

第二节 56-60 DEABC 61-65 JIFGH

第三节 66-70 BCAED

第三部分

第一节 71. smartphone 72. inventions 73. chief 74. difficulties 75. interest

第二节 76. interested 77. chatting 78. smoking 79. remembered 80. happier

第三节 81. C 改为 is spent 82. A 改为 to get 83. A 改为 not
         84. D 改为 painting/to be painted 85. A 改为去掉 was

第四节 书面表达

Mobile Payment

Nowadays, mobile payment is becoming more and more popular in our shopping.

In my opinion, compared with those traditional ways, mobile payment is faster and more convenient. Besides, it can be used at any time and any place. So we can save a lot of time by mobile payment.

Furthermore, mobile payment needs a phone and a network. When we use it, we should have a password. To protect our money, we shouldn't give our password to others.

With the help of mobile payment, we can buy something without cash. It makes our life more convenient. It plays an important role in our daily lives.